Humility in the Writings of Charles Wesley and the Early Church Fathers/Mothers

Humility in the **Writings** of **Charles Wesley** and the **Early** Church Fathers/Mothers

BY S T Kimbrough, Jr.

FOREWORD BY
John H. Erickson

WIPF & STOCK · Eugene, Oregon

HUMILITY IN THE WRITINGS OF CHARLES WESLEY AND THE
EARLY CHURCH FATHERS/MOTHERS

Wipf & Stock
An Imprint of Wipf and Stock Publishers
199 W. 8th Ave., Suite 3
Eugene, OR 97401

www.wipfandstock.com

PAPERBACK ISBN: 979-8-3852-2720-4
HARDCOVER ISBN: 979-8-3852-2721-1
EBOOK ISBN: 979-8-3852-2722-8

VERSION NUMBER 09/11/24

"There is more value in a little study of humility and in a single act of it than in all the knowledge in the world."

—St. Teresa of Avila

Contents

Foreword

HUMILITY IS A PARADOXICAL virtue, and also an elusive one. Jokes abound about monastics or otherwise virtuous people arguing about who is more humble. Their pretentions may not be as phony as those of Uriah Heep in Dickens's *David Copperfield*, but by boasting of their humility or simply by calling attention to it in some less conspicuous way, they show themselves to be other than humble. To use a catchy neologism, they "humblebrag." To gain facility in this, they make use of self-help books and career coaches who offer advice on strategies for cultivating and maintaining a humble mindset—something widely regarded these days as necessary for success in business, leadership, and life. Entrepreneurs excel in projecting a winsome just-folks demeanor. They are proud of their humility—exactly the paradoxical situation that Charles Wesley explores so brilliantly in his verse and experiences in his own struggle with humility and pride.

No one is better qualified than S T Kimbrough to explore the study of humility as we meet it in the writings of Charles Wesley and in the fathers and mothers of early church. I remember with gratitude the consultations that he convened at St. Vladimir's Seminary and elsewhere in the early 2000s that gathered musicians, theologians, patristic scholars, and church leaders from across Wesleyan and Orthodox traditions to explore commonalities and areas of convergence. Both traditions are rooted in Scripture, read attentively and in its entirety. Both speak of participation in divine life, sanctification, *theosis*. Both meditate upon the sublime paradox of the Incarnation and celebrate it in hymns of joyous wonder. Both espouse an eschatological vision that is at once humbling and hopeful: We look forward with faith and hope to a new age that comes into being through Jesus Christ, crucified, risen, and glorified, of which we can have a foretaste even in this present age. Participants in those stimulating conversations gained a deeper appreciation of the faith that we hold in common as well as a clearer understanding of issues that may still divide us.

As I write these words, the Orthodox Church is approaching the fourth Sunday of Lent, which is devoted to the memory of St. John Climacus, seventh-century abbot of St. Catherine's monastery at the foot of Mount Sinai and author of *The Ladder of Divine Ascent*, a classic of Orthodox spirituality. The spiritual ladder that he writes of has thirty steps. These correspond (if we follow Luke 3:23) to the approximate age of Jesus when he began his three years of public ministry. Luke of course tells us a good deal more about the early "hidden" years of Jesus' life. If the story of his encounter with the elders in the Temple at age twelve offers any indication, Jesus may have been less meek and mild than we sometimes imagine. In any case, the thirty steps of *The Ladder of Divine Ascent* offer an expansive account of what happened when, after his baptism, Jesus "full of the Holy Spirit, returned from the Jordan, and was led by the Spirit for forty days in the wilderness, tempted by the devil" (Luke 4:1–2 RSV).

The author of the *Ladder* speaks on such temptations out of his own monastic background, but he is writing for Everyman/Everywoman. At the thirtieth rung of the *Ladder*, we reach three virtues that bind them together in unity—faith, hope, and love— but the greatest of these is love" (1 Corinthians 13:13), for God himself is love (1 John 4:8). Certainly this sums up the teaching of Orthodox spirituality, from the Desert Fathers through our own times. It also sums up the teaching—and the poetry—of Charles Wesley.

In this study of humility S T touches on two further issues that challenge our churches today, one involving political theology, the other involving liturgical theology and, more generally, the place of the church's worship in the formation of our spiritual lives. Sustained involvement in political and social issues of the day and systematic reflection on them is not something for which Orthodox Christians are well known, at least on a corporate level. S T devotes an entire chapter to a noteworthy exception, St. Basil the Great, whom he brings into dialogue with Charles Wesley. There are indeed congruences in their thought as well as in their engagement with social issues. "Be thankful and humble, but never be still," writes Wesley. As S T remarks, this line "does not sound like a quotation from the Desert Fathers." Very true! But St. Basil had nearly a decade of "desert" experience behind him before his bishop persuaded him to be ordained as a priest, and he was notably zealous even before that, from the time of his Christian conversion and baptism (as a young adult) onward. Whether this was always a "humble zeal" is less easy to determine. It certainly did have political and social implications.

While not well known for social action or contributions to political theology, the Orthodox are deservedly famous for their liturgical worship and piety. Here S T offers an intriguing suggestion. If, as St. Basil says, "everything that Christ did was a lesson in humility," S T asks, could it be that "the liturgy of the church is a means of practicing humility?" The cycle of the church year does indeed offer many lessons in humility drawn from the life of Christ. These may "precipitate the overt life of humility's practice . . . without conscious awareness of performance." The practice of humility may in this way become second nature for us, "habitual" to use the standard technical term for such indwelling, in this way opening "an option to personify and realize a humble life beyond liturgy" (p. 89).

But in our liturgical observances we may encounter some hidden temptations. Many of us have deep emotional reactions as we participate in the services of the Christmas cycle, of Lent, of Holy Week and the Easter cycle, and other observances of the liturgical year, but it is easy to lose sight of their inner cohesion. We may become more attached to one liturgical cycle or celebration than to another. Or we may end up treating them as successive episodes in the biography of Jesus during his life on earth—a big mistake! Along the way, we can easily forget the mystery of Christ in all its fullness, the mystery of Christ as we meet it in the *kenosis* hymn of Philippians 2:6–11.

Orthodox priests are reminded of this mystery whenever they pick up a typical hand cross from the altar table. It is double sided, with the crucifixion on one side, Christ rising in glory on the other, and the superscription "King of Glory" on both. This leads us to some basic questions. What is the relationship between historical commemoration and eschatological expectation? The relationship between looking back at Jerusalem in the time of Christ and looking ahead to a heavenly Jerusalem? The relationship between remembering times and places of the past, and being molded here and now by God's kingly rule? It is hard—conceptually—to hold together the mystery of our salvation, but hold it together we must, just as we hold it together when we pick up a two-sided liturgical cross. I am grateful that S T Kimbrough has come to help us once again as we ponder such questions and as we try to grasp that cross. May we do this with humble zeal!

Fr. John H. Erickson

Peter N. Gramowich Professor of Church History Emeritus and former Dean
St. Vladimir's Orthodox Theological Seminary
Yonkers, NY

Technical Notes Regarding Texts of Charles Wesley Included in This Volume

1. The eighteenth century was a time of important changes in the English language. Many transitions were being made from old Anglo-Saxon spelling and punctuation, as well as printing practices. Charles Wesley's writing spans the period from 1738 to 1788, the year of his death. His writing in the second half of that century reflects the acceptance of some of the language changes taking place. For example, *Hymns for the Nativity of Our Lord* (1745) was published twenty-six times during Charles's lifetime. The last printing was in 1788. Notice the following changes in verb spellings between 1745 and 1788: reconcil'd = reconciled; shew'd = showed; ador'd = adored. In the edition of 1788, apostrophes for the past tense of verbs ('d) are changed to "ed." To what extent Charles Wesley himself made these changes is reflected in some of his latest manuscripts, though most of the changes would become the practice of Charles Wesley's printers. For instance, the capitalization of nouns, except for names and proper nouns, tends to fade from practice. Charles Wesley's verse cited in this volume reflects these changes. When "ye" is used for the second person "you," this change is made. His use of "thee," "thou," and "thine" in reference to God, and his use of old forms of some words, such as "goest," "hast," "hath," "wast," etc., remain unchanged.

2. Throughout this volume some words and phrases of Wesley's poetry expressly related to the discussion of humility are often italicized. Occasionally Wesley italicized words for emphasis, and these are retained.

Abbreviations

LXX   Septuagint, sometimes known as the Greek Old Testament or the translation of the Seventy, hence the abbreviation LXX. It is the earliest Greek translation of the Hebrew Bible.

Wesley, Charles

FH 1759   *Funeral Hymns.* London: [Strahan], 1759.

HGEL 1742   *Hymns on God's Everlasting Love.* London: Strahan, 1742.

HFC 1763   *Hymns for Children.* Bristol: Farley, 1763.

HNL 1745   *Hymns for the Nativity of Our Lord.* London: [Strahan], 1745.

HSP 1749   *Hymns and Sacred Poems.* 2 Vols. Bristol: Farley, 1749.

RH 1747   *Hymns for Those That Seek and Those That Have Redemption in the Blood of Christ.* London: Strahan, 1747.

SH 1762   *Short Hymns on Select Passages of the Holy Scriptures.* 2 Vols. Bristol: Farley, 1762.

Thanksgiving Hymns 1759   *Hymns to Be Used on the Thanks-*
        giving Day, Nov. 29, 1759, and After it. [London:
        Strahan, 1759].

UP 2   *The Unpublished Poetry of Charles Wesley.* Vol. 2.
        Eds. S T Kimbrough, Jr., and Oliver A. Becker-
        legge. Nashville: Abingdon/Kingswood, 1990.

UP 3   *The Unpublished Poetry of Charles Wesley.* Vol. 3.
        Eds. S T Kimbrough, Jr., and Oliver A. Becker-
        legge. Nashville: Abingdon/Kingswood, 1992.

Wesley, John, and Charles Wesley

HSP 1739   *Hymns and Sacred Poems.* London:
        Strahan, 1739.

HSP 1740   *Hymns and Sacred Poems.* Bristol: Farley, 1740.

HSP 1742   *Hymns and Sacred Poems.* Bristol: Farley, 1742.

HLS 1745   *Hymns on the Lord's Supper.* Bristol: Farley, 1745.

Wesley, John

CPH 1743   *A Collection of Psalms and Hymns Published by*
        John Wesley, M. A. Fellow of Lincoln College, Ox-
        ford; and Charles Wesley, M. A., Student of Christ-
        Church, Oxford. 2nd ed. London: Strahan, 1743.

1780 *Collection*   *A Collection of Hymns for the Use of the People*
        Called Methodists. Eds. Franz Hildebrandt and
        Oliver A. Beckerlegge. Works of John Wesley,
        Vol. 7. Oxford: Oxford University, 1983.

Introduction

IN 1999 THE OFFICE of Mission Evangelism of the General Board of Global Ministries of The United Methodist Church, of which I was the director, and St. Vladimir's Orthodox Theological Seminary jointly convened the first of four consultations on the theme of "Orthodox and Wesleyan Spirituality" with participants from the following traditions: Greek Orthodox, Russian Orthodox, Bulgarian Orthodox, the Orthodox Church in America, the British Methodist Church, the Methodist Church in Singapore, The United Methodist Church, the Nazarene Church, and the Roman Catholic Church. "The primary themes addressed by the presenters had to do with holiness and perfection, the impact and influence of the East in the writings of John and Charles Wesley, the founders of Methodism, and the common and foundational ground on which the Wesleys and many of the eastern Fathers stood."[1]

Many valid questions were explored regarding an effective methodology for studying the theology and spirituality of the early Church Fathers/Mothers and other leading theologians from a different era, indeed centuries apart. Father Thomas Hopko, a distinguished New Testament scholar and Dean of St. Vladimir's Orthodox Theological Seminary at the time of the first consultation on "Orthodox and Wesleyan Spirituality," eloquently summarized its importance.

> Whatever the influences of early Eastern Christian writers on the Wesley brothers' doctrine and hymnody

---

1. Kimbrough, *Orthodox and Wesleyan Spirituality*, 11.

1

(which, as every teacher knows, cannot be determined simply by counting references in writings), the essays in this volume clearly demonstrate that what informed, instructed, and inspired the Orthodox church fathers and their disciples and John and Charles Wesley and their companions was exactly the same. These were men and women bound to God's Word recorded in the Bible and recapitulated in Christ crucified. They read, prayed, preached, and lived this Word, personally and in community, as called, chosen, and faithful people justified, sanctified, and glorified by the one God and Father and his only Son Jesus Christ, God's incarnate Word, and the one Holy Spirit. They were witnesses and worshippers of the Holy Trinity, one in nature and undivided.

What can be learned about Christian faith and life in the original sources and authoritative witnesses of Eastern Orthodoxy and Wesleyan Methodism is boundlessly enlightening and life-giving. We thank God for raising up Christian scholars capable of offering these theological and spiritual treasures. We also thank these scholars for accepting their calling and fulfilling it so well.[2]

The second consultation on "Orthodox and Wesleyan Spirituality" with the theme "Worship and Devotional Life in the Orthodox and Wesleyan Traditions" was held at Trinity College, June 16–20, 2000, in Bristol, UK. The third consultation convened at the Orthodox Spiritual Academy in Crete, Greece, August 1–7, 2002, addressed the theme "Holy Scripture in the Orthodox and Wesleyan Traditions." The presentations from these consultations were combined and published in the volume *Orthodox and Wesleyan Scriptural Understanding and Practice*.[3] The fourth consultation was held at St. Vladimir's Orthodox Theological Seminary, January 8–13, 2006. Its theme was "One, Holy, Catholic, and Apostolic Church: Ecclesiology and the Gathered Community." The presenters' lectures were published in a third volume, *Orthodox and Wesleyan Ecclesiology*.[4]

2. Kimbrough, *Orthodox and Wesleyan Spirituality*, 8–9.
3. Kimbrough, 2005.
4. Kimbrough, 2007.

Growing out of my study of Charles Wesley's extensive literature over against the vast literature of Eastern Christianity, one theme has kept surfacing with considerable regularity, namely, the many congruences in the doctrine of *theosis* so dominant in the theology of the early Church Fathers/Mothers and in the theology of the Wesleys, and Charles Wesley in particular. This resulted in my exploration of this subject in the volume *Partakers of the Life Divine: Participation in the Divine Nature in the Writings of Charles Wesley*.[5] At the end of that volume I made reference to the *Philokalia*, an extensive collection of texts from Eastern Christianity, which is seen by some as a hermeneutical filter of Orthodox thought and beyond, i.e., for other traditions. In a similar manner I suggested that the extensive literature of Charles Wesley, in similar manner, serves as a hermeneutical filter of Wesleyan thought and beyond for other traditions.

In the current volume I have turned once again to the *Philokalia* and other sources as a reservoir of eastern theology against which to mirror Charles Wesley's theology of humility. Again the congruences are amazing.

There is one other publication that resulted directly from my study of the encounter of Charles Wesley's theology with that of the Eastern Church Fathers and Mothers, namely, "Charles Wesley and a Window to the East"[6] in *Charles Wesley: Life, Literature & Legacy*. There are a number of scholars who have opened this window a little wider: Albert Outler,[7] Ted A. Campbell,[8] Frances Young,[9]

---

5. Kimbrough, *Participation in the Life Divine*, 2016.

6. Chapter by S T Kimbrough, Jr., 165–83.

7. See the following: *The "Platonism" of Clement of Alexandria* (1940); *Augustine: Confessions and Enchiridion*, 1955; *The Christian Tradition and the Unity We Seek*, 1957; *Historian and Interpreter of Christian Tradition*. Vol. 9, 1995.

8. Ted A. Campbell. *John Wesley and Christian Antiquity*, 1999.

9. Frances Young. "Inner Struggle: Some Parallels between the Spirituality of John Wesley and the Greek Fathers" in *Orthodox and Wesleyan Spirituality*, 157–72. Also, "God's Word Proclaimed: The Homiletics of Grace and Demand in John Chrysostom and John Wesley," in *Orthodox and Wesleyan Scriptural Understanding and Practice*, 137–48.

Gordon Wakefield,[10] A. M. Allchin,[11] Geoffrey Wainwright,[12] Michael Christensen,[13] Nicholas Lossky,[14] Kenneth Carveley,[15] John Chryssavgis,[16] Peter Bouteneff,[17] James H. Charlesworth,[18] Tamara Grdzelidze,[19] John A. Jillions,[20] and others. The Russian Orthodox priest and educator Ioann Ekonomtsev asserts that "one should stress the great importance of the Wesley phenomenon [particularly Charles in his view] as an important spiritual bridge between the two related cultures of the East and West."[21]

This study continues the exploration of Charles Wesley's thought, namely his ideas on the subject of humility in relation to

10. Gordon S. Wakefield. "John Wesley and Ephraem Syrus," 8, 12. "Littérature du desert chez John Wesley," 1978.

11. A. M. Allchin, *Participation in God: A Forgotten Strand in Anglican Tradition*, 1988.

12. Geoffrey Wainwright. "Trinitarian Theology and Wesleyan Holiness" in *Orthodox and Wesleyan Spirituality*, 59–80.

13. Michael J. Christensen and J. Wittung, eds. *Partakers of the Life Divine*, 2007.

14. Nicholas Lossky, "Lancelot Andrewes. A Bridge between Orthodoxy and the Wesley Brothers in the Realm of Prayer," in *Orthodox and Wesleyan Scriptural Understanding and Practice*, 149–56.

15. Kenneth Carveley. "From Glory to Glory: The Renewal of All Things in Christ: Maximus the Confessor and John Wesley," in *Orthodox and Wesleyan Spirituality*, 173–88.

16. John Chryssavgis. "The Practical Way of Holiness: Isaiah of Scetis and John Wesley," in *Orthodox and Wesleyan Spirituality*, 81–99.

17. Peter C. Bouteneff. "All Creation in United Thanksgiving: Gregory of Nyssa and the Wesleys on Salvation," in *Orthodox and Wesleyan Spirituality*, 189–201.

18. James H. Charlesworth. "Two Similar Paths: Methodism and Greek Orthodoxy," in *Orthodox and Wesleyan Scriptural Understanding and Practice*, 107–29.

19. Tamara Grdzelidze, "The Authority of Scriptural Interpretation: An Orthodox Perspective on the Positions of John Wesley and Modern Methodism," in *Orthodox and Wesleyan Scriptural Understanding and Practice*, 131–36.

20. John A. Jillions. "An Orthodox Reading of 1 Cor. 1:10–30: Any Room for Methodists?" In *Orthodox and Wesleyan Scriptural Understanding and Practice*, 43–63.

21. "Charles Wesley and the Hesychast Tradition," in *Orthodox and Wesleyan Spirituality*, 240.

many important thinkers of eastern Christianity, particularly St. Basil the Great. As emphasized by Thomas Hopko, it is the shared tradition of being rooted in Holy Scripture, whose truth is realized in Christ's crucifixion, a truth the faithful seek to actualize both personally and corporately through prayer, proclamation, and as witnesses to the ever-living Holy Trinity, Father, Son, and Holy Spirit, that makes the shared theological enquiries viable. Such study may not, however, excise the early Church Fathers and Mothers or the Wesleys from their historical contexts, for their emerging thought always has a historical locus.

The discovery of much commonality in the Wesleyan and Orthodox quest for holiness in recent years,[22] which is at the heart of their theological identity, emphasizes the importance of beginning with the roots of their faith and history as other facets of theology are examined.

"God resists the proud, but gives grace to the humble" (James 4:6). Humility is a central focus of Scripture and of Charles Wesley in his poetry and sermons through which one grasps the central foci of his theology and its relationship to the theology of the early Church Fathers and Mothers.

"Charles Wesley's theological views remain relatively unknown, and there is much to be done."[23] While it is in his poetry that one often elucidates his theological views in the turn of a phrase, a lyrical homiletical narrative, or an exposition of a biblical passage, there is an interesting prose explication of humility in his sermon on Psalm 126, which is crucial to the understanding of his perspective(s) on humility, especially as it is explored in relationship to the witnesses of the early Church. Here is an important excerpt from that sermon.

---

22. See a series of chapters in *Orthodox and Wesleyan Spirituality*: Chapter 3, Geoffrey Wainwright, "Trinitarian Theology and Wesleyan Holiness;" Chapter 4, John Chryssavgis, "The Practical Way of Holiness: Isaiah of Scetis and John Wesley;" Chapter 5, Petros Vassiliadis, "Holiness in Perspective of Eucharistic Theology;" Chapter 6, Dimitar Kirov, "The Way of Holiness."

23. Newport, *The Sermons of Charles Wesley*, 53.

Let us now consider this great truth a little more particularly. The first of all Christian graces and the foundation of all is humility: a deep sense of our spiritual poverty, a feeling knowledge that we are nothing but sin and deserve nothing but shame. And a clear sight that we have nothing and can do nothing no, not so much as think a good thought. And is such a virtue as this the seed of joy? Yea, as surely as it is the seed of all other virtues. As surely as it is contrary to pride which is the seed of all torment. No sooner does humility enter a soul, which before was all storm and tempest, but it says to that sea "Peace, be still," and there is a great calm. There is indeed in every branch of humility a sweetness which cannot be uttered. There is pain, 'tis true, in the entrance into it, but that very pain is full of pleasure. There is mourning joined with it; but even that mourning is blessedness; it is health to the soul, it is marrow to the bones. It heals while it wounds; it delights at the same time and in the same degree wherein it softens the heart. Humility not only removes all that pain and anguish with which pride drinks up the blood and spirits; it not only plants peace wherever it comes, and brings rest to the weary soul; but joy too and such joy as together with increases it more and more unto the perfect day.

Humility cannot but lead to faith: a sight of our disease makes us soon fly to the cure of it. Who can feel himself sick and not long to be made whole? What contrite sinner is not glad of a saviour? And he is the more glad, the more firmly he believes, that he is able and willing to save to the uttermost; able to save all that can believe, for he is God! And willing, for he is man! Here is joy! Joy which none can divide from faith! Joy unspeakable and full of glory! God, the Lord God, Jehovah, God over all, the God to whom all things are possible, hath undertaken the cause of lost man! He hath promised, he hath sworn to save them! . . . Yea, tell it out in all the lands! God hath died! He hath died to save man! Let the heavens rejoice, and the earth be glad. Publish ye, praise ye, and say, this is the victory which overcometh the world, even our faith. If we can believe, all things are possible to him that believeth: to him it is easy, "to rejoice evermore"! Yea, he cannot but rejoice in thy strength, O Lord Christ, and be exceeding glad of thy salvation![24]

For Charles Wesley humility plays an active role in the process of salvation. It "can but lead to faith." This is a foundation of his theology to be discovered in the exploration of his works, particularly in relation to the saints and witnesses of the early Church. This emphasis on the relationship of humility and salvation recalls the words of Thomas à Kempis from his fifteenth-century classic *Humility and the Elevation to the Mind of God:* "Without humility, there is no salvation nor real virtue."[25]

Charles's many uses of the words "humble" and "humility" stress the importance of the humble posture of the followers of Jesus. This issues in large measure from his grasp of the humbleness of Jesus. It is important to understand two aspects of Charles Wesley's vocabulary of humility: his use of the word "humble" as an adjective and his use of adjectives that modify the noun "humility." Chapters 2, 3, and 4 of this study are concerned with *humble* love, the *humble* heart, and *humble* faith. However, we also encounter such language as humble caution, humble mind, humble confidence, humble zeal, humble thankfulness, and humble joy. Some examples of the adjectives modifying "humility" addressed here are: meek humility, unfeigned humility, active humility, true humility, just humility, and concealed humility. In Wesley's theological language it is apparent that the adjective "humble" and the noun "humility" pervade almost every aspect of human character, personality, and experience. This is an outgrowth of a theology of *theosis*,[26] which, in Charles's view, pervades every dimension of

24. Newport, *The Sermons of Charles Wesley,* 127–28. This is one of his sermons that illustrates his views on humility.

25. *Humility and the Elevation,* 3.

26. See Michael J. Christensen's discussion of John Wesley's formulation of a doctrine of entire sanctification and its parallels with a patristic concept of *theosis*. "Wesleyan sanctification appears as a domesticated (or democratized) version of the more ancient doctrine." *Partakers of the Life Divine,* 223. As A. M. Allchin has shown, however, Charles's view of sanctification, or in this instance deification, was rooted in an earlier view of deification exemplified in the writings of Gregory of Nazianzus. See Allchin's *Participation in God: A Forgotten*

human experience, for since God is love, the divine embodies all dimensions of humility. Since God, who as Charles states "is humility," imparts the divine nature of love to the faithful, human beings are the recipients of God's humble love. Thus, they are to embody divine love which itself is the essence of humility.

Charles Wesley truly believed that the humble person attributes nothing to himself. In the course of this study we will discover how Wesley's concept of humility intersects with the Holy Scriptures and the witnesses of the early Church.

Dietrich von Hildebrand has summarized a view of humility that is closely akin to that of Charles Wesley. "Humility does not prevent a person from seeing that, with God's help, he[/she] has been making progress in some direction; but he[/she] must never lose sight of the essential relativity of that progress. The determination never to cease advancing—a process that has no end in this life—is one of the basic conditions of holiness."[27]

There is an extended transcription in Charles Wesley's hand[28] of portions of *Sentimens de Piété* (1713) of François de Salignac de la Mothe (1651–1715), which contains a section on "False and Real Humility" with which Wesley probably would have concurred.

> It is false humility to believe ourselves unworthy of God's goodness and to not dare to look to him with trust. True humility lies in seeing our own unworthiness and giving ourselves up to God, never doubting that he can work out the greatest results for and in us. If God's success

---

Strand in Anglican Tradition. The opening couplet of a hymn from *HSP* 1739 Allchin finds most convincing: "Heavenly Adam, Life Divine, / Change my nature into thine" (stanza 11, 221). In the *1780 Collection* "Adam" is changed to "Father." Charles did not share John's view of possible entire sanctification in this life. This is clear from John's letters to Charles, and Charles's volumes, *SH* 1762, in which he asserts a view of gradual sanctification whose fulfillment or realization occurs at the time of death. Rather than affirm a specific appropriation of an Orthodox theology of *theosis*, Randy Maddox prefers to speak of finding in Wesleyan theology "significant parallels with the Eastern Orthodox theme of deification (*theosis*)." *Responsible Grace*, 122.

27. von Hildebrand. *Humility: Wellspring of Virtue*, 76.

28. This French-language document in Charles Wesley's hand writing may have resulted from Charles working with John Fletcher to improve the former's knowledge of the French language.

depends on finding our foundations already laid, we might well fear that our sins had destroyed our chances. But God needs nothing that is in us. He can never find anything there except what he himself has given us. No, we may go further and say that the absolute nothingness of the creature, bound up as it is with sin in a faithless soul, is the fittest of all subjects for the reception of his grace. He delights to pour it out on such souls, for sinful souls who have never experienced anything but their own weakness cannot claim any of God's gifts as their own possession. It is just as St. Paul says, "God chose the foolish things of the world to shame the wise."[29]

Unquestionably Charles Wesley understood that there was such a thing as false humility and real humility. First and foremost, he believed that humility was intimately related to the nature of God. In *SH* 1762 Charles reflected on Psalm 136:1, "The Lord is good, his mercy endureth forever," and wrote:

> *Thy nature doth itself impart*
> *To every humble longing heart;*
> And all that after thee aspire
> Shall gain with thee their whole desire,
> United to their source above,
> Lost in a boundless sea of love.[30]

Here *theosis* is a key to the understanding of the humble heart. To receive the humble heart means to receive the nature of God. The divine nature is imparted to "every humble longing heart." Therefore, it is God who imparts humility. We do not make ourselves humble on our own. All that human beings desire should be involved with aspiring to divine humility. They are "united to their source." What is this source?—"a boundless sea of love." Humility is thus intimately related to God's nature, divine love.

Similarly, Wesley prays in *HSP* 1740:

---

29. Edmonson and Helms. *The Complete Fénélon*, 9. It is of particular interest that in practicing his French language Charles Wesley copied portions of Fénélon's works including this passage.

30. *SH* 1762, 1:279; based on Psalm 136:1, "The Lord is good, his mercy endureth forever" (KJV).

> Plant in us thy humble mind;
> Patient, pitiful, and kind,
> Meek, and lowly let us be,
> Full of goodness, full of thee.[31]

The humble mind has the likeness of Christ which is implanted within. Its virtues are those of the mind of Christ: patient, pitiful, kind, meek, lowly, full of goodness, but most of all "full of thee."

Stanza 8 from the familiar hymn "O for a heart to praise my God" also emphasizes that in *theosis* there is the fullest expression of humility in humankind and its intimate relationship with divine love. Charles writes:

> Thy nature, dearest Lord, impart,
>   Come quickly from above,
> Write thy new name upon my heart,
>   Thy new, best name of love.[32]

God's nature that is imparted to human beings is humble love. Or as Charles writes on another occasion in speaking of the second person of the Trinity, "Thou art all humility."[33] The essence of God is perhaps best described by the word humility. Thus, he writes in volume 2 of *HSP* 1749: "Gentle thou, and meek in heart, / All humility thou art," from a poem based on Matthew 11:28–30, particularly the words, "Come unto me—learn of me," etc. Further, responding to the simple phrase, "Learn of me" in Matthew 11:29, Wesley pens these words:

> Lord, I fain would *learn* of thee
> *Meekness and humility*;
> In thy gentleness of mind,
>   In thy lowliness of heart
> Rest mine inmost soul shall find,
>   Rest that never can depart.[34]

---

31. *HSP* 1740, 183.

32. *HSP* 1742, 31.

33. *HSP* 1742, 195. This is the same text from which the familiar hymn, "Gentle Jesus, meek and mild," comes.

34. *SH* 1762, 2:162; based on Matthew 11:29, "Lean of me" (KJV).

These are most interesting words, for one does not usually think of a didactic process whereby one learns of humility. Nevertheless, Wesley is reminding his readers that, though some persons seem by their very nature to embody the quality of humility, one can indeed "learn of humility," and, in this instance from Christ. It is not surprising that in his *Hymns for Children* (1763) this theme surfaces: "Meek, and lowly may I be, / Thou art all humility."[35] Charles envisions humility as being learned by children. Learning of and receiving the nature of God means that we are "Rooted in humility," and the constant prayer is what Wesley anticipates for children as they grow, namely that they may possess a "meek and lowly mind."

> Rooted in humility,
> Still in every state resigned,
> Plant, Almighty Lord, in me
> A meek and lowly mind.[36]

Throughout his poetry Charles focuses on the words humble and humility in many different ways. Just as a jeweler turns a diamond stone in the light and sees multiple refractions of light, so Charles speaks, as mentioned at the beginning of this introduction, of the humble heart, humble faith, humble love, humble zeal, humble confidence, humble love, humble poor, humble caution, humble care, and the humble, active mind. The following chapters will examine these concepts throughout his poetry and where possible show how many of them interface with the early witnesses of the Church.

In matters related to humility it is appropriate to comment that Charles in large measure agreed with the interpretation of humility by his brother John with one exception. Charles spoke of "concealed humility" and "silent love," in other words, humility is a very private matter and needs no public affirmation. John, however, spoke of a "voluntary humility" that might prevent followers of Christ from claiming Christian perfection or witnessing about it to others.[37]

35. *HFC* 1763, 21.
36. *HFC* 1763, 21.
37. See below page 45, footnote 26.

Chapter 1: The Origin of Humility

God Is Humility

THE INCARNATION IS EVIDENCE of the self-humbling of God. Through divine initiative there is a divestment of God's eternal majesty, as God comes to live among the creatures of creation. In one of his hymns on the nativity Ephrem the Syrian[1] (c. 306–373) reminds us of the self-humbling of God.

> He [was] wrapped [in] swaddling clothes in *baseness*,
> But they offered him gifts.[2]

The Incarnation is the revelation of God's humility. What does Ephrem mean with the word "baseness"? Certainly any child could be wrapped in swaddling clothes, and tightly bundled after birth. But being placed in a manger in an animal stall is the birthplace for God's own Son. Certainly this is a sign of humble beginnings of the Christ Child.

Charles Wesley says something quite similar in a poem based on Luke 2:7, but which was not published during his lifetime.

> See, you blushing sons of pride,
> See your God a child become!

1. Also known as Ephrem of Edessa or Aprem of Nisibis, he was a distinguished theologian and hymnographer of Eastern Christianity. He is venerated as a saint in the Eastern Orthodox Church and in other churches. His works of hymns, poems, sermons in verse, and prose exegesis of Scripture passages are highly valued in church history.

2. McVey, *Ephraim the Syrian Hymns*, Hymn 23, stanza 12, 129.

When He would on earth reside,
    Earth can scarce afford him room:
Wrapped himself in swaddling bands
    Who with darkness swathes the sea,
Who the universe commands,
    Comprehends immensity!

Triumph we, the sons of grace,
    That our God is born so poor,
Doth his majesty abase
    Our salvation to secure:
Glorying in our Infant-King,
    Him we in the manger own,
Him whom highest seraphs sing
    High on his eternal throne.[3]

In another hitherto unpublished poem during his lifetime based on Luke 2:12, Charles speaks of sharing in the life of God "by humility alone."

Is this, O Lord, the sign
    That makes thy Greatness known,
The ornament of power Divine,
    The glory of thy throne?
    Ennobled by thy birth
    My faith the manger sees,
And all the precious things on earth
    Are vile, compared to this.

'Tis here thy mind I know,
    Thy hidden kingdom see;
Thou com'st from heaven to reign below
    By deep humility;
    The High and Lofty One
    Thou dost our meanness bear:
And *by humility alone*
    Thy royal state we share.[4]

3. *UP* 2:79; based on Luke 2:7, "And she brought forth her firstborn son, and wrapped him in swaddling clothes, and laid him in a manger; because there was no room for them in the inn" (KJV).

4. *UP* 2:79–80; based on Luke 2:12, "And this shall be a sign unto you; you

That one shares God's "royal state" *by humility alone* is reminiscent of the comment by Amma Syncletica of Alexandria[5] (d. 373): "Just as one cannot build a ship unless one has some nails, so it is impossible to be saved without humility."[6] Similarly St. Mark the Monk affirmed, "Unless a man gives himself entirely to the cross, in a spirit of humility . . . he cannot become a true Christian."[7]

In a poem found in the same unpublished manuscript by Wesley just cited, he asks a question that he is forever asking throughout his life.

> And shall the ransomed sons of men
> *God in his humbled state* disdain,
> The manger, as the cross, despise,
> Or stumble at their Maker's cries?[8]

There is also a stunning and eloquent statement on God's humility by Charles Wesley in his little volume of *Hymns for the Nativity of Our Lord*, when he writes of God the Maker who is "Emptied of his Majesty, / Of his dazzling glories shorn."

> Him the angels all adored
>   Their Maker and their King:
> Tidings of their *humbled Lord*
>   They now to mortals bring:
> Emptied of his majesty,
>   Of his dazzling glories shorn,
> Being's *source begins to* be,
>   And God himself is born![9]

---

shall find the babe wrapped in swaddling clothese, lying in a manger" (KJV).

5. Amma Syncletica of Alexandria is a Christian saint and one of the desert mothers known by the name "Amma," some of whose sayings survive.

6. Ward, *The Sayings of the Desert Fathers*, 235.

7. Ware, *The Orthodox Way*, 129. St. Mark the Monk, born in Athens, is also known as Mark the Ascetic, a fifth century theologian. He is considered a saint in the Eastern Orthodox Church and author of numerous works on the spiritual life.

8. *UP* 2:80; Luke 2:13, "And suddenly there was with the angel a multitude of the heavenly host praising God" (KJV).

9. *HNL* 1745, 6.

Humility's origin resides in God's humble love, for God is love. As Ilia Delio states: "Humility is not a quality of God, it is an essential aspect of God's nature as love."[10] Charles Wesley affirms that we know of God's humility through the God-Child Jesus. Ephrem the Syrian also states that Jesus was born humble:

> The womb of your mother overthrew the orders:
> The Establisher of all entered a Rich One;
> He emerged poor. He entered her a Lofty One;
> *He emerged humble.* He entered her a Radiant One,
> And He put on a despised hue and emerged.[11]

Jesus emerged humble at his birth, God's ultimate example of humility.

Charles Wesley is very clear about the origin of humility in a poem he wrote based on Matthew 11:28–29, "Come to me, all you that are weary and are carrying heavy burdens, and I will give you rest. Take my yoke upon you, and learn from me; for I am gentle and humble in heart, and you will find rest for your souls" (NRSV).

> Lovely Lamb, I come to thee,
> Thou hast oft invited me;
> Surely now I would be blest,
> Give me now the promised rest.

> All my business and concern
> Is of thee, my Lamb, to learn;
> Show me thy lesson first show,
> Now alas! I nothing know.

> Gentle thou, and meek in heart,
> *All humility thou art;*
> Full of wrath, and pride I am,
> How unlike my lowly Lamb!

> But thou canst my soul transform,
> Humble an aspiring worm,

10. Delio. *The Humility of God,* 5.
11. McVey. *Ephrem the Syrian Hymns.* 11:7, 1–6, 132.

My unbroken spirit break,
Make the angry leopard meek.[12]

Charles is clear—God is humility, "All humility thou art." And God
has the capacity to turn the prideful to the humble: "thou canst
my soul transform." He would perhaps agree with St. Francis' (b.
?–1226) affirmation of God as "sublime humility" as expressed in
his "Letter to the Entire Order."

> O wonderful loftiness and stupendous dignity!
> O *sublime humility*
> O *humble sublimity!*
> The Lord of the universe
> God and the Son of God,
> so humbles himself
> that for our salvation
> He hides Himself
> under an ordinary piece of bread!
> Brothers, look at the *humility of God*
> and *pour out your hearts before Him!*
> Humble yourselves
> That you may be exalted by Him!
> Hold nothing back of yourselves for yourselves
> That he who gives himself totally to you
> may receive you totally.[13]

In a text published in *HSP* 1742, Charles strongly affirms that
God is "all humility." These words appear in his familiar text of
"Gentle Jesus, meek and mild" in which he writes as though these
are the words of a child. Here are stanzas 8 through 10 of the poem.

> Lamb of God, I look to thee,
> Thou shalt my example be,
> Thou art gentle, meek, and mild,
> Thou wast once a Little Child.

---

12. *HSP* 1749, 2:161; stanzas 1–4 of an eight-stanza hymn, based on Matthew 11:28–30.

13. Francis of Assisi. "A Letter to the Entire Order," in Delio. *The Humility of God*, 29–30.

Fain I would be, as thou art,
Give me thy obedient heart;
Thou art pitiful and kind,
Let me have thy loving mind.

Meek, and lowly may I be,
Thou art all humility;
Let me to my betters bow,
Subject to thy parents thou.[14]

Of course, the text refers specifically to Jesus, but as an integral part of the Trinity, for Charles understands that Jesus is God.

Feeling and Learning Humility

In *HSP* 1749, Charles expressed the desire, in a classic Wesleyan phrase, to *feel* God's humility.

O my dear Master, and my Lord,
    Good is thine acceptable will,
I yield obeisance to your word,
    I come, *your humbled state to feel,*
My calling here I plainly see
To bear, and bleed, and die with thee.[15]

Wesley makes clear that this is not merely a "feel good" way of somehow experiencing the humility of God. There is a process of learning. Charles reads the simple words in Matthew's Gospel, "Learn of me" (11:29) and writes:

Lord, I fain would learn of thee
Meekness and humility;
In thy gentleness of mind
    In thy lowliness of heart
Rest mine inmost soul shall find,
    Rest that never can depart.[16]

14. *HSP* 1742, 195.

15. *HSP* 1749, 2:18.

16. *SH* 1762, 2:162; based on Matthew 11:29, "Take my yoke upon you, and learn of me" (KJV).

How does one learn meekness and humility?—from the example and words of Jesus, from his parables and the Sermon on the Mount, from him upon the cross.

Nevertheless, humility is not merely something to be learned. It also involves God's activity in us. In Charles's early reflections on the Psalms, particularly Psalm 131, he writes of the psalmist's ponderings on not having an aspiring heart and eyes for higher things. Yet Charles has somehow come to quiet trust and knows that his aspirations and response need the imparting of God's grace.

> Lord, if thou the grace impart,
> Poor in spirit, meek in heart,
> I shall as my Master be
> Rooted in humility.[17]

In his volume *The Tree of Life* St. Bonaventure[18] (1221–1274) claims that:

> humility is the root and guardian of all virtues. By this statement he meant that Christian life must be grounded in humility if God is to be the center of life. By "humility" Bonaventure meant a self-knowledge grounded in truth, patience with others, simplicity of life, attentive listening to others, courage to overcome temptations and a compassionate heart. . . . Yet, humility is not a virtue we strive for.[19]

Humility becomes the foundation of one's life just as it is in the life of Christ.

Wesley emphasizes again the vital importance of God's role in being rooted in humility.

> Save me from wrath, the plague expel;
> Jesu, thy humble self impart;

---

17. *CPH* 1743, 95.

18. St. Bonaventure, born Giovanni di Fidanza, was of the Franciscan order and an Italian bishop, cardinal, theologian, and philosopher, who sought to integrate faith and reason.

19. Delio, *The Humility of God*, 129.

O let thy mind within me dwell;
O give me lowliness of heart.[20]

When Charles prays: "O let thy mind within me dwell; / O give me lowliness of heart," one is reminded of Paul's words, "Let this mind be in you, which was also in Christ Jesus" (Philippians 2:5 KJV).

But what is humility? St. John Climacus[21] (c. 579–c. 649) helps one to respond to this question in his work, *The Ladder of Divine Descent.*

> Let all who are led by the spirit of God enter with us into this spiritual and wise assembly, holding in their spiritual hands the God-inscribed tablets of knowledge. We have come together, we have investigated, and we have probed the meaning of this precious inscription. And one man said: "It [humility] means constant oblivion of one's achievements." Another: "It is the acknowledgment of oneself as the last of all and the greatest sinner of all." And another: "The mind's recognition of one's weakness and impotence." Another again: "In fits of rage, it means to forestall one's neighbor and be first to stop the quarrel." And again another: "Recognition of divine grace and divine compassion." And again another: "The feeling of a contrite soul, and the renunciation of one's own will." But when I listened to all this and had attentively and soberly investigated it, I found that I had not been able to attain to the blessed perception of that virtue from what had been said. Therefore, last of all, having gathered what fell from the lips of those learned and blessed fathers as a dog gathers the crumbs that fall from the table, I too gave my definition of it and said: "Humility is a nameless grace in the soul, its name known only to those who have learned it by experience. It is unspeakable wealth, a name and gift from God, for it is said: 'learn not from an angel, nor from man, nor from a book, but from Me, that is,

20. *HSP* 1740, 69.

21. John Climacus was a sixth–seventh century monk also known as John of the Ladder, who was part of the Monastery of Mount Sinai. He is known as an author from the Hesichast tradition and particularly his work *The Ladder of Divine Ascent.*

from My indwelling, from My illumination and action in you; for I am meek and humble in heart and in thought and in spirit, and your soul shall find rest from conflicts and relief from thoughts."[22]

Wesley's well-known and beloved hymn which is a prayer, "Love divine, all loves excelling," opens with a similar request, i.e., for God's indwelling and illumination:

Love divine, all loves excelling
    Joy of heaven, to earth come down,
Fix in us thy humble dwelling,
    All thy faithful mercies crown.[23]

Fr. Theoklitos of Dionysiou[24] asks, "How can we make Christ come and dwell in our hearts? How else, except through love?"[25]

Clothed in Humility

There is an interesting metaphor that Charles uses in reference to the importance of God's humility. He wishes to be clothed with God's holiness, which he equates with humility: "Clothe me with thy holiness, / Thy meek humility."

Jesu, full of truth and grace,
    In thee is all I want:
Be the wanderer's resting-place,
    A cordial to the faint;
Make me rich, for I am poor,
In thee may I my Eden find,
    To the dying health restore,
        And eye-sight to the blind.

22. Climacus, *The Ladder of Divine Ascent*. Step 25: "On the Destroyer of the Passions, Most Sublime Humility, Which is rooted in Spiritual Perception."

23. *RH* 1747, 11.

24. Fr. Theoklitos of Dionysiou was a twentieth-century monk of Mount Athos.

25. Ware, *The Orthodox Way*, 41.

Clothe me with thy *holiness,*
    Thy meek humility,
Put on me thy glorious dress,
    Endue my soul with thee;
Let thy image be restored,
Thy name, and nature let me prove,
With thy fullness fill me, Lord,
    And perfect me in Love.[26]

Humility is the "glorious dress" of God. One bears humility in one's demeanor, on one's countenance, and in one's body language, in one's whole being. One becomes evidence of the restored image of God and hence is being perfected in love. Charles's equation of holiness and humility is encountered elsewhere in his writings.

Evagrius the Solitary[27] (345–399) also speaks of the importance of being clothed in reverence and humility. "If a man, still enmeshed in sin and anger, does shamelessly to reach out for knowledge of divine things . . . such a soul . . . ought to be clothed in due reverence and humility."[28] If indeed, we are clothed in humility, this is the nature of God that is imparted to us in Christ. St. Philotheos of Sinai[29] (9th or 10th century) emphasized: "Our Lord Jesus Christ, being God incomprehensible, unknown and ineffable, wishing to show us the way of eternal life and holiness, was clothed in humility during his whole life in the flesh."[30]

St. Isaac the Syrian[31] (613–700) speaks of humility in a similar manner as the "raiment of the Godhead."

---

26. *HSP* 1742, 45.

27. Evagrius was an influential and highly regarded theologian from the fourth century. He was an ascetic monk from Heraclea, a city located on the coast of Bithynia in Asia Minor.

28. *Philokalia,* 1:70.

29. St. Philotheos of Sinai was head of the St. Catherine Monastery on the Sinai Peninsula. His forty texts on *Watchfulness* are included in the *Philokalia.*

30. *Philokalia,* 3:20.

31. St. Isaac the Syrian, a seventh-century Syriac Christian theologian and bishop, also known as Isaac of Nineveh, is remembered for his works on Christian asceticism.

Humility is the raiment of the Godhead. The Word who became human clothed himself in it, and he spoke to us in our body. Everyone who has been clothed with humility has truly been made like unto Him who came down from his own exaltedness and hid the splendor of his majesty and concealed his glory with humility, lest creation be utterly consumed by the contemplation of him.[32]

Thus to be clothed with humility is to be clothed with the "raiment of the Godhead." Is our humility to be visible? In a prayer of St. Symeon the New Theologian[33] (949–1022) one prays for God to observe or see one's humility.

See my humility!

See each of my labors and all of my sins!
Absolve me, O God of all, that with a pure heart,
    Trembling thoughts and a contrite soul
I may partake of thine undefiled and most holy Mysteries
    Which enliven and deify all who partake of
    Them with a pure heart.[34]

As we reflect on God *being* humility and the human attempt to learn humility and to become humble, St. John Climacus offers these thought-provoking words: "It is one thing to be humble, another to strive for humility, and another to praise the humble. The first belongs to the perfect, the second to the truly obedient, and the third to all the faithful."[35]

---

32. See website: www.glory2godforallthings.com, accessed January 28, 2024. See further Hilarion Alfeyev. *The Spiritual World of Isaac the Syrian.*

33. St. Symeon the New Theologian is one of three saints of Eastern Christianity (including John the Apostle and Gregory of Nazianzus) given the title "theologian." His discourses and poems on the spiritual life emphasized that mystically and directly one could experience God's presence.

34. *Service Books of The Orthodox Church.* Vol. 1. *The Divine Liturgy of St. John Chrysostom,* 116. The prayer is titled the "Sixth Prayer of St. Simeon the New Theologian."

35. *Service Books of The Orthodox Church.* Vol. 1. *The Divine Liturgy of St. John Chrysostom,* 116.

John Chrysostom[36] (347–407) "There are many kinds of humility: one is humble in his own measure, another with all excess of lowliness. . . . The sacrifice for God is a contrite spirit, a contrite and an humble heart God will not despise."[37]

In the *Philokalia* we read: "All of our holy fathers knew this and all with one accord teach that perfection in holiness can be achieved only through humility. Humility, in its turn, can be achieved only through faith, fear of God, gentleness and the shedding of all possessions. It is by means of these that we attain perfect love through the grace and compassion of our Lord Jesus Christ, to whom be glory through all the ages. Amen."[38]

36. John Chrysostom is a very important early church father who served as the bishop of Constantinople. He was particularly well known for his preaching and his liturgical legacy, namely the Divine Liturgy of Saint John Chrysostom. An extremely prolific author including hundreds of exegetical homilies on Old and New Testament texts, he is recognized as a saint in the Eastern Orthodox Church and many other churches.

37. John Chrysostom's *Homily 15 on Matthew*. Advent: https://www.newadvent.org/fathers/200115.htm; accessed February 11, 2024.

38. Ibid., 93.

Chapter 2: **Humble Love**

God Is Humble Love

IT IS THE IMPARTING of God's nature that fills the human heart with love. It is unquestionably a humble love. Charles uses the adjective "humble" to describe what Scripture avers is God's nature, namely love. Is there a need to speak of God's love as humble, if love is who God is, and God's love is constant? Human beings, particularly because of their sinful nature, tend to create diverse dimensions of love. They find many ways of expressing love, many of which need the influence of humility.

In a poem titled simply "Submission," Charles prays for the mysterious union with God. "Let the manner be unknown, / So I may with thee be one." Since God's nature is revealed as love ("God is love," 1 John 4:8), union with God means union with divine love. The heights of holiness Charles understands to be "all the depths of humble love." Holiness and divine or humble love are understood as one and the same.

> So may I thy Spirit know,
> Let him as he listeth blow,
> Let the manner be unknown,
> So I may with thee be one.
> Fully in my life express
> All the heights of holiness,
> Sweetly in my spirit prove
> All the depths of *humble love*.[1]

1. *HSP* 1742, 153.

The idea of oneness with the divine is at the heart of the concept of *theosis,* an ongoing emphasis of Charles Wesley. He realizes, however, that the "manner" or "process" of becoming one with God is "unknown." The interesting stanza above is from a poem published in *HSP* 1742. Within eight lines he brings together the concepts of holiness, humility, divine image, God's nature, and love, which culminate in the hope: "perfect me in love." Since God by nature is humble love, when our natures are joined with God, we become humble love, and holiness embodies our being. It is our spiritual clothing.

In the following text, cited previously, Charles makes the daring plea, "Let thy image be restored, / Thy name and nature let me prove." Dare one think of the possibility that a human being can be the proof in this world of God's nature? Charles Wesley does.

> Clothe me with thy holiness,
>   Thy *meek humility,*
> Put on me thy glorious dress,
>   Endue my soul with thee;
> Let thy image be restored,
> Thy name and nature let me prove,
>   With thy fullness fill me, Lord,
>   And *perfect me in love.*[2]

Another interesting poem written by Charles is titled "Written in Going to Wakefield to Answer a Charge of Treason." When he once fervently preached for God to bring back the banished, some interpreted this to mean that he was endorsing bringing back the Pretender[3] to the English throne. He was not speaking politically, however, but spiritually—*all of the banished of the earth* should return or turn to God. Nevertheless, being charged, he had to travel to Wakefield to "Answer a Charge of Treason." Therefore, Charles wrote:

> Jesu, in this hour be near,
>   On thy servant's side appear,

2. *HGEL* 1742, 45.

3. Someone who claims to be the legitimate sovereign, though someone else occupies the throne.

Called thine honor to maintain,
Help a feeble child of man.

Thou who at thy creature's bar,
Didst thy deity declare,
Now my mouth and wisdom be,
Witness for thyself in me.

Gladly before rulers brought,
Free from trouble as from thought,
Let me thee in them revere,
Own thine awful minister.[4]

In this difficult moment of his life Charles sought to walk the simplest of spiritual paths, that of "simple faith and humble love." The poem continues:

All of mine be cast aside,
Anger, fear, and guile, and pride,
Only give me from above,
Simple faith, and *humble love*.[5]

Though his vision is simply articulated, fulfilling it was no easy task, as he described time after time.

The Depth of Humble Love

Charles elaborates on the importance of *humble love* in the lives of Jesus' followers. In one of his "Hymns for the Use of the Methodist Preachers" he asserts that the Methodist preachers are "meekly safe in humble love," because they are "fixed on the Rock" (Jesus) and are united in mind and spirit with one another.

Wherefore to thine almighty hand
    The keeping of our hearts we give,
Firm in one mind and spirit stand,
    To thee, and to each other cleave,

4. *HSP* 1749, 2:239; stanzas 1–3 of a six-stanza poem.
5. *HSP* 1749, 2:239.

> Fixed on the Rock which cannot move,
> And meekly safe in *humble love*.[6]

There is a poem titled "After a Recovery" in volume 1 of *HSP* 1749, in which Charles avers that the height of perfection is "the depth of humble love."

> Assert thy claim, receive thy right,
> Come quickly from above,
> And *sink* me to perfection's *height*,
> The *depth* of *humble love*.[7]

What a fascinating concept so eloquently articulated: "And *sink* me to perfection's *height*, / The *depth* of humble love." Perfection's height would seem to be a noble goal to which one ascends in this life. But Wesley says, No. You reach perfection's height only by sinking to "the depth of humble love."

The constant prayer of Charles is that anything that would cause him to stray from humble love be removed from his path, so that he will not stumble. He knows that stumbling can transpire daily, and that he is never without the need for the following prayer:

> For this we strive, for this we pray,
> Take the stumbling-block away,
> The cursed thing remove.
> Uphold, and make our footsteps sure,
> And let us stand, and walk secure
> In *humble faith, and love*.[8]

In Hymn VII of "Hymns for the Watch-Night" published in *HSP* 1749, he speaks of coming to the conclusion of his earthly race and rendering up his final breath. He desires to do so "in humble love and fear." Thus he will regain the divine image.

---

6. *PW* 6:100; see also manuscript Miscellaneous Hymns.

7. *HSP* 1749, 1:164.

8. *HSP* 1749, 2:28.

Thus let me pass my days
Of sojourning beneath,
And languish to conclude my race,
And render up my breath,
In *humble love* and fear,
Thine image to regain,
And see thee in the clouds appear,
And rise with thee to reign.[9]

In a text to which he gives the title "The Preacher's Prayer for the Flock" in his "Hymns for the Use of the Methodist Preachers" Charles Wesley addresses those who are perverse and seek to divide the church through greed, pride, and lies. He pleads, "Ah! Never suffer them to leave, / The church where thou art pleased to give / Such tokens of thy grace." He says that humble love is the protection of the congregations. Such is its power: it embodies "the strength of all-sufficient grace." This strength is received in diverse ways that God appoints, and this strength ultimately leads to eternal life.

What then can their protection be?
The virtue that proceeds from thee,
The power of *humble love*:
The strength of all-sufficient grace,
Received in thine appointed ways,
Can land them safe above.[10]

Though Wesley speaks of the "power of humble love," when he wrote about the death of a Mrs. Lefevre, who died at the young age of thirty-three, he was overcome by what he saw in her as a love-perfected life. He eloquently describes her lamb-like spirit thus: one "who was bestowed with love invincible, love which turns the other cheek, love that is meek and bears and conquers all things."[11]

As he so often does in his death poems that remember the faithful who are examples of how to live the Christian life, he speaks of the humble love of Mrs. Lefevre as being "simplified."

9. *HSP* 1749, 2:128.
10. "Hymns for the Use of the Methodist Preachers," 1760, 21.
11. Kimbrough, *May She Have a Word with You?* 37.

> Like her, who now supremely blest,
> Enjoys an everlasting rest,
>   We fain on earth would be;
> As harmless as that gentlest dove,
> As simplified as *humble love*,
>   As perfectly like thee.[12]

United with God in Humble Love

After reading the story of Enoch's union with God in Genesis 5:22, "Enoch walked with God" (KJV), Charles wrote a poem of eight lines in which he asserts that through *humble love* we are united with God. He senses that humble love links him to God. It is this linkage which sees him through the worst of times: "Through the fire, or through the sea." He longs for companionship with Jesus, namely, that he would be joined to him through "humble love."

> O that I might walk with God!
>   *Jesus* my companion be,
> Lead me to thy blest abode,
>   Thro' the fire, or thro' the sea:
>
> *Joined to thee by humble love*
>   Nothing I desire beside,
> Only let me never move,
>   Never stir without my guide.[13]

Though the implication might seem to be that this transpires only when we are finally taken into God's presence, that is not Charles's intention here. He has affirmed that in baptism we have become partners with God. In one of his baptismal hymns he states, "Thy nature, Lord, through faith I feel." We are recipients of God's nature, and thus we become stewards of divine love. Humble love perhaps expresses, as well as Charles can, the love that unites us with God.

---

12. *FH* 1759, 49; On the Death of Mrs. L[efevre], July 6, 1756.

13. *SH* 1762, 1:14; based on Genesis 5:22, "Enoch walked with God" (KJV).

How is faith to be measured?—"by soberness of humble love." He is very clear that we are not good measurers of our own faith, for we cannot say that we have *humble love*. His response to Romans 12:3 makes this very apparent, particularly stanza 3.

Jesus, to me vouchsafe the grace
  Of jealous self-mistrusting fear,
And then the vigilant faithfulness
  To warn thy flock of danger near,
That all may cautiously go on,
Nor glory in a state unknown.

Not one of all thy saints but needs
  The warning salutary word:
Ev'n grace the pride of nature feeds,
  Forgetful of our gracious Lord
If once we in *our* gifts delight,
And arrogate the giver's right.

Wherefore let every soul beware,
  Nor think above what God hath done,
Nor pompously his state declare,
  But magnify the Lord alone,
And thus his faith's true measure prove
By *soberness of humble love.*[14]

The Eucharist and God's Humble Love

A discussion of humble love cannot be concluded without a reference to the Eucharist. "The way to contemplate the mystery of God's humble love, according to Francis, is in the Eucharist."[15] It is precisely the "mystery of God's humble love" that Charles Wesley contemplates in many of his texts on the Eucharist in *HLS* 1745.

---

14. *SH* 1762, 2:284–85; based on Romans 12:3, "I say, through the grace given unto me, to every man that is among you, not to think of himself more highly than he ought to think; but to think soberly, according as God hath dealt to every man the measure of faith" (KJV).

15. Delio, *The Humility of God*, 29.

> Amazing mystery of love!
>> While posting to eternal pain,
> God saw his rebels from above,
>> And stooped into a mortal man.
>
>   . . .
>
> Jesu, our pardon we receive,
>> The purchase of that blood of thine,
> And now begin by grace to live,
>> And breathe by breath of love divine.[16]

Quite specifically Charles reflects on the love with which the Eucharist fills the worshiper at the table of the Lord.

> With bread from above,
> With comfort and love
> Our spirit he fills,
> And all his unspeakable goodness reveals.
>
> O that all men would haste
> To the spiritual feast,
> At Jesus's word
> Do this, and be fed with the love of our Lord.[17]

Charles punctuates this reality further by saying "We shall his choicest blessings taste, / And banquet on his richest love."[18] The Eucharist is the feast of feasts that fills us with divine love.

> O what a soul-transporting feast
>> Doth this communion yield!
> Remembering here thy Passion past
>> We with thy love are filled.[19]

At the Lord's table—

> Love's mysterious work is done;
> Greet we now th' atoning Son,
> Healed and quickened by his blood,
> Joined to Christ, and one with God.[20]

16. *HLS* 1745, Hymn 36, p. 27; stanzas 1 and 4 of a four-stanza hymn.

17. *HLS* 1745, Hymn 92, p. 79; stanzas 7–8 of a twelve-stanza hymn.

18. *HLS* 1745, Hymn 93, p. 81; lines 5–6 of stanza 2.

19. *HLS* 1745, Hymn 94, p. 82; stanza 1 of a four-stanza hymn.

20. *HLS* 1745, Hymn 164, p. 137; stanza 3 of an eight-stanza hymn.

Chapter 3: The Humble Heart

INTERTWINED WITH THE CONCEPT of humble love is Wesley's idea of the humble heart. Following a number of Scripture passages, Wesley sees the heart as the seat of human emotions and feeling. In *HSP* 1742 he published eloquent prayers for humility. In stanzas 1, 2, 8, and 9 of the text quoted below he prays for the gift of the "humble heart."[1] He desires that the locus of human emotion above all else be humble. If God fills the faithful with the divine nature, which is love and of which Charles speaks as humble love, it follows naturally that those filled with humble love will be imbued with a humble heart. He pleads, "Show me what in Christ thou art" and in so doing "Give me, Lord, an humble heart." "The fathers also say that we cannot fully acquire the virtue of purity unless we have first acquired real humility of the heart."[2]

The Hardened Heart

> O my Father, and my God,
>   Look upon thy helpless child!
> Thou hast laid aside thy rod,
>   Thou in Christ art reconciled:
> Hear me then, my Father, hear,
>   Good, and gracious as thou art,
> Fill me with an holy fear,
>   *Give me, Lord, an humble heart.*

1. *HSP* 1742, 148–50.
2. *Philokalia*, 1:77.

O! 'Tis all I want below,
    Jesus, and myself to feel,
Only sin, and grace to know,
    All the good and all the ill.
Show me, Father, what I am,
    Show me what in Christ thou art,
All my glory, all my shame;
    Give me, Lord, an humble heart.

Listen to my ceaseless cries,
    Mean and little may I be,
Base, and vile in my own eyes,
    Grieved at my own misery.
Show, and then my sickness cure;
    Make me know as I am known,
Wound my spirit, make me poor,
    Break, O break this heart of stone.

Dust and ashes is my name,
    Sinful dust and ashes I
Back return from whence I came,
    Earth to earth I sink, and die.
Abject I, yet haughty too,
    Nothing of my own possess,
Nothing of myself can do,
    Proud of sin, and proud of grace.

O the curse, the plague I feel
    By the demon pride pursued!
Proud to see I merit hell,
    Proud I am that God is good,
Proud, that thou my works hast wrought,
    Proud that I was justified,
Proud in every word and thought:
    All my fallen soul is pride.

My own glory still I seek,
    Still I covet human praise,
Still in all I do, or speak,
    Thee I wrong, and rob thy grace:

34

Nature will usurp a share,
    Fondly of thy graces boast,
Needlessly thy gifts declare,
    Needlessly declared and lost.

And must that which is so good
    Evil prove to helpless me?
Poison shall I draw from food,
    Sin from grace, and pride from thee?
O forbid it humble love!
    Hide me, O my Father, hide,
Far away this snare remove,
    Save me from the demon pride.

Wean my soul, and keep it low,
    Do not with thy gifts destroy,
Lowliness of heart bestow,
    Give me this, or take my joy:
If with me thou wilt not stay,
    Let my comfort all depart,
Take my joy, and peace away,
    Leave me but an humble heart.

Father hear, to thee I cry,
    Thee in Jesu's name conjure,
With my own request comply,
    Make me humble, make me poor;
This of all thy gifts impart;
    When I am of this possessed,
When thou giv'st an humble heart,
    If thou canst, withhold the rest.[3]

Charles speaks of his own heart, as does the prophet Ezekiel, as consisting of stone, and prays that it will be broken.
Throughout the poem Charles writes in the first person. Stanza
6 sounds like an honest confession: "My own glory still I seek,
/ Still I covet human praise, / Still in all I do, or speak, / Thee I
wrong, and rob thy grace." He is convinced that his own pride
can "rob [God's] grace." He is willing to forego all gifts in life

3. *HSP* 1742, 148–50.

except the "humble heart." Just as the prophet Ezekiel wishes to have his heart of stone removed (36:22–26, especially "It is the Lord God who promises to remove the heart of stone from the house of Israel"), so Wesley prays:

> "Break, O break this heart of stone."

Here one sees that confession and humility are closely related. Stanza 3 shows how both are related to self-esteem. Even if Wesley sees himself as "mean, little, base and vile" in his own eyes, and grieved at his own misery, he prays that God will "Make me know as I am known." How is he known by God? He is known as a sinner, redeemed by love, who has received the nature of God, which is love. Hence, low self-esteem is transformed into an understanding of self that embodies the love of God. Thus, he is content with the humble heart.

God Imparts the Humble Heart

What are then the characteristics of the contrite heart of which one needs to be aware? Reflecting on Psalm 51:10, "Create in me a clean heart, O God; and renew a right spirit within me" (KJV), Wesley describes in stanzas 3 and 4 of the familiar hymn "O for a heart to praise my God"[4] the kind of humble heart he desires.

> An *humble, lowly, contrite heart,*
>   Believing, true, and clean,
> Which neither life nor death can part
>   From him that dwells within.
>
> An heart in every thought renewed,
>   And full of love divine,
> Perfect, and right, and pure and good,
>   A copy, Lord, of thine.

The heart is full of divine love, hence, it is humble, lowly, and contrite. Charles's statement concerning a "heart in every

---

4. *HSP* 1742, 31.

thought renewed" reminds one of a statement in volume 1 of the *Philokalia*: "When the intellect prays without distraction it afflicts the heart; and 'a broken and contrite heart, O God, you wilt not despise'" (Ps. 51:17).[5] Further, Nikitas Stithatos[6] (c. 1005–1090) avers: "Humility is not achieved by means of a scraggy neck, squalid hair, or filthy, ragged and unkempt clothing, to which the generality of men ascribe the sum total of this virtue. It comes from a heart and a spirit of self-abasement. As David said, 'God will not scorn a contrite spirit, and a contrite and humble heart' (cf. Ps. 51:19, LXX)."[7]

I have noted earlier the importance of stanza 8, the last stanza, of Wesley's hymn "O for a heart to praise my God" for the concept of *theosis*.

> Thy nature, dearest Lord, impart,
>   Come quickly from above.
> Write thy new name upon my heart,
>   Thy new, best name of love.

When God's nature [LOVE] is imparted, divine love creates the humble heart. The previous four lines are a prayer pleading for the imparting of God's nature. Is the person of faith acting too boldly in requesting to be imbued with God's nature? Who can ask this of God? Inspired by the following words from 1 Kings 3:5, "God said, Ask what I shall give thee" (KJV), Wesley penned lines that reflect the humble desire to know God as intimately as possible.

> Thou bidst me ask whate'er I will,
>   Thou wilt the thing required bestow:
> I ask thy hallowing Spirit's seal,
>   I ask, thy precious self to know,
> I ask an humble, perfect heart,
>   With all thou hast, and all thou art.[8]

5. *Philokalia*, 1:128.

6. Stithatos, a Byzantine mystic and theologian, was a follower of Symeon the New Theologian and is considered a saint by the Eastern Orthodox Church. He wrote some hundred texts on the practice of the virtues.

7. *Philokalia*, 4:114.

8. *SH* 1762, 1:165–66; based on 1 Kings 3:5, "God said, Ask what I shall

In another text he emphasizes that God's nature is indeed imparted to those of a "humble longing heart." Those who seek God with a humble heart will be united with God and "lost in a boundless sea of love."

> Full of unutterable grace
> Jesus mine eye of faith surveys!
> Jesus, whate'er thou art is mine.
> Fountain of excellence divine!
> All goodness is comprised in thee,
> Good in thyself, and good to me.

> *Thy nature doth itself impart*
> *To every humble longing heart;*
> And all that after thee aspire
> Shall gain with thee their whole desire,
> United to their Source above,
> Lost in a boundless sea of love.[9]

Examples of the Humble Heart, Indwelled Yet Unfinished

In his poems on women of the Bible, Wesley singles out Mary and Martha in what I have called the Martha-Mary formula.[10] He sees in them the virtues of contemplation and active service, which he desires for himself, as expressed in the following lines from *RH* 1747.

> Lo! I come with joy to do
>   The Master's blessed will,
> Him in outward works pursue,
>   And serve his pleasure still;
> Faithful to my Lord's commands,
>   I still would choose the better part,
> Serve with careful Martha's hands,
>   And *humble* Mary's heart.[11]

---

give thee" (KJV).

9. *SH* 1762, 1:279; based on Psalm 136:1, "The Lord is good, his mercy endureth forever" (KJV).

10. See Kimbrough, *May She Have a Word with You?* 5.

11. *RH* 1747, 7.

Here we see Charles's vision of how the humble heart and active service are bound together. Actually, he says that one *serves* "with careful Martha's hands, / And humble Mary's heart." The humble heart is not passive; it serves.

A constant theme of Charles Wesley is that God "indwells" us and as he does so, the human heart is the seat of God's presence within. He is humbled by the thought that God vouchsafes to dwell within us, a gift which transpires by God's grace. It is God who imparts "the humble, poor, and broken heart."

> Beyond the bounds of space and time
> On his eternal throne sublime,
> Will God's most glorious majesty
> Vouchsafe to cast a look on me?
> Yes, if to me his grace impart
> The humble, poor, and broken heart,
> The holy, high, and lofty One
> Shall make my heart his earthly throne.[12]

Nevertheless, Charles does not perceive the humble heart as an accomplished state. It is an ongoing process.

> Author of faith, eternal word,
>   Whose Spirit breathes the active flame,
> Faith, like its Finisher and Lord,
>   Today, as yesterday the same;
>
> To thee our humble hearts aspire,
>   And ask the gift unspeakable:
> Increase in us the kindled fire,
>   In us the work of faith fulfill.[13]

God's Spirit is ever in motion and "breathes the active flame." Thus, Wesley prays using two active verbs: "increase," and "fulfill," i.e., "Increase in us the kindled fire, / In us the work of faith fulfill." If the fire within is to be increased and there is yet more work of faith to fulfill, by no means can the idea of the humble

---

12. *SH* 1762, 1:370, based on Isaiah 57:15–17; stanza 1 of a three-stanza poem.

13. *HSP* 1740, 6; stanzas 1 and 2 of a six-stanza poem.

heart be a completed state. It is an ongoing process throughout the Christian's life. The humble heart increases, grows! It does not maintain a status quo. As the early fathers maintained: "Just as snow will not produce a flame, or water a fire, or the thorn-bush a fig, so a person's heart will not be freed from demonic thoughts, words, and actions until it has first purified itself inwardly, uniting watchfulness with the Jesus Prayer, attaining humility and stillness of soul, and eagerly pressing forward on its path."[14]

The Path Toward the Humble Heart

Wesley understands that the path toward the humble heart involves repentance and an experience of Christ's dying love.

> Savior, Prince enthroned above,
> Repentance to impart,
> Give me through thy dying love
> The *humble contrite heart*.[15]

Notice that Wesley uses an additional adjective, "contrite," often used by the early church fathers, to express the intensity of the meaning of a humble heart. He uses this same phrase "An humble contrite heart" again in one of the "Hymns for One Fallen from Grace."

> O that I could repent,
> With all my idols part,
> And to thy gracious eye present
> An *humble contrite heart!*
> An heart with grief oppresst
> At having grieved my God.
> A troubled heart that cannot rest
> 'Till sprinkled with thy blood![16]

As individual and corporate as the idea of the humble heart may be for Charles regarding the life of the individual Christian

14. *Philokalia.* 1:182.

15. *HSP* 1749, 1:121.

16. *HSP* 1749, 1:143.

and the church, the body of Christ, there is a broader cosmic dimension of which he speaks. God's Incarnation in itself has cosmic dimensions, as angels announce God's breaking into human existence through the birth of the God-Child Jesus. There is a cosmic dimension to God's redemptive work in the Incarnation. Charles Wesley understands this as well in God's earthly presence in Jesus and in the indwelling of the humble heart in God's earthly children, for it fills earth and heaven. He writes:

> He did: the King invisible,
> Jehovah, once on earth did dwell,
>   And laid his majesty aside:
> Whom all his heavens cannot contain,
> For us he lived, a mournful man
>   For us a painful death he died.

> Still the great God resides below,
> (And all his faithful people know
>   He will not from his church depart)
> The Father, Son, and Spirit dwells,
> His kingdom in the poor reveals,
>   And *fills with heaven the humble heart.*[17]

"If the humility of God is really all about the Incarnation, then we must admit that the humility of God involves our lives as well because we are members of the Body of Christ. . . . The humility of God must shine through our lives if the evolution of the universe is to progress toward its completion in Christ."[18]

How then will Charles prepare his heart so that it is the ongoing dwelling of Christ? Very early in his ministry he concludes that it must be prepared with sincere and genuine humility or "by unfeigned humility."

> Oft I in my heart have said,
>   Who to the deep shall stoop,
> Sink with Christ among the dead

---

17. *SH* 1:167; based on 1 Kings 8:27, "But will God indeed dwell on the earth?" (KJV).

18. Delio, *The Humility of God*, 131.

From thence to bring him up?
Could I but my heart prepare
By *unfeigned humility,*
Christ would quickly enter there,
And ever dwell with me.[19]

19. *HSP* 1742, 179.

Chapter 4: Humble Faith

Faith and Humility

DOES ONE THINK OF faith as bearing the quality of humility? Can faith be proud? If faith involves complete trust, how can one speak of faith itself as humble or proud? One speaks of a person of faith and of followers of Jesus as congregations or communities of the faithful. Indeed the misguided faithful can be proud and devoid of humility. But can faith demonstrate humility? This depends on those who seek to live by faith. Are there not those who have the opportunity to show that living by faith means living humbly? Faith and humility go together. In Charles's understanding and in that of the early Fathers, you cannot have one without the other.

Charles Wesley turns to examples in Scripture of those who demonstrate humble faith in their lives. Of Noah's behavior in preparing for the ensuing flood, he writes:

> Divinely warned of judgments near,
>   Noah believed a threat'ning God,
> With *humble faith*, and holy fear
>   He built the ark, and 'scaped the flood.[1]

Those who live as persons of faith are to do it humbly. They are to actualize humble faith. St. Mark the Ascetic[2] sees the "unity of

---

1. *HSP* 1740, 9.

2. Mark the Ascetic was also known as St. Mark the Monk; see see footnote 7 on page 3.

faith and humility," perhaps as a synonym for humble faith and exemplary of a life posture.

> Bring before your eyes the blessings, whether physical or spiritual, conferred on you from the beginning of your life down to the present, and call them repeatedly to mind in accordance with the words: 'Forget not all his benefits' (Ps. 103:2). Then your heart will readily be moved to the fear and love of God, so that you repay him as far as you can, by your strict life, virtuous conduct, devout conscience, wise speech, true faith and humility—in short by dedicating your whole self to God.[3]

Nevertheless, one can in no way anticipate the results of what it means to live by and with humble faith. This is reserved only for divine knowledge.

> Eye hath not seen, ear hath not heard,
> By heart conceived it cannot be,
> The bliss thou hast for him prepared,
> Who waits in *humble faith* for thee.[4]

Humble faith anticipates a life lived in service to God at all costs, and anticipates no return. "Eye hath not seen, ear hath not heard, / By heart conceived it cannot be"[5] KJV.

Thus humble faith becomes the posture of daily living and of worship before God. It is the posture of prayer. Life by humble faith foresees no easy path.

> But lo! With *humble faith* I bow
> My soul before thy throne:
> Deliver me from evil now;
> For thou canst save thine own.[6]

Charles pleads for deliverance from evil in a world of temptation in eighteenth-century England which is his context. When one reads his political verse, one is immediately aware of the diverse

3. *Philokalia*, 1:152.

4. *HSP* 1740, 201.

5. See 1 Corinthians 2:9.

6. *HSP* 1749, 1:201.

controlling and opposing forces in English society that pitted the aristocracy against the poor. When he pleads "Uphold, and make our footsteps sure," is he speaking only in spiritualized terms devoid of association with reality? He had experienced the horrors of slavery in the American colonies. Could he ever cast this out of his mind as an evil, or a "cursed thing," or as evidence of the "cursed thing"? Notice particularly the two stanzas which precede Charles's use of this term. Yes, there is a war that "subsists within," a war from which he pleads, "Save, O save us, Lord."

> Thou God of love, and truth, and power,
>   Guard us in the evil hour,
>   By sore temptation tried.
> Shelter thy poor, afflicted flock,
> And in the clefts of Israel's Rock,
>   Our trembling spirits hide.
>
> Long as the war subsists within,
>   Save, O save us, Lord, from sin,
>   The lusting flesh subdue;
> The Spirit's stronger lust exert,
> And watch o'er every helpless heart,
>   Till thou hast made us new.
>
> For this we strive, for this we pray,
>   Take the stumbling-block away,
>   The cursed thing remove,
> Uphold, and make our footsteps sure,
> And let us stand, and walk secure
>   In *humble faith*, and love.[7]

Does "the stumbling-block . . . the cursed thing" refer only to the condemnation of the fall of Adam and Eve? Can it have a much broader meaning? In any case, Charles desires a sure footing for his stance and walk through life, and above all that he walks "In *humble faith*, and love." The addition of the word "love" to "humble faith" seems almost redundant. But is it redundant? Perhaps Charles is simply punctuating the meaning of humble

7. *HSP* 1749, 2:28.

faith with the word "love," for to walk securely in humble faith means to walk imbued with God's nature, love.

Humble Faith for One and All

One must carefully reflect on Charles's use of *humble faith*, for it is not merely an expression used from an individual perspective. He uses it both individually and corporately. He writes with "humble faith *I* bow / *My* soul before thy throne, / Deliver *me* from evil now." Clearly he is here concerned with the individual's response to God. In the poem last quoted, however, he uses a plural pronoun: "guide us . . . save us." In his lyrical commentary on the Scriptures published in 1762, he speaks of *humble faith* in a very strong corporate sense.

> By *humble faith* and active love
> Long as we stay with thee,
> Thou wilt not from *thy church* remove,
> Thou wilt abide with me.
>
> With thee that I may still remain,
> And never more depart,
> Jesus, create my soul again,
> And dwell within my heart.[8]

The people of God, the church, are challenged to be as faithful as is God. The church abides with God and God abides with the church. The church does so by *humble faith* and *active love*, an indispensable pair, each expressing the other. It is claimed, however, that "Humility is not action, nor a sequence of actions, nor a habit formed by the repetition of actions. It is, rather, a receptivity or passivity; a matter of being acted upon by God."[9] Though humility is a life posture exemplified by and learned from Jesus, it is intimately linked with active love, for God's love is not static. Humility motivates the implementation of God's love for all creation.

8. *SH* 1:202–03, based on 2 Chronicles 15:2, "The Lord is with you, while ye be with him" (KJV).

9. M. Casey, *Living in the Truth*, 56.

"All created reality expresses in some way the humility of God."[10] Hence Wesley speaks of humble faith as issuing from the humility of God and being intimately joined with active love which can have important results for a follower of Jesus.

Humble faith is an author of patience. It enables one's patience. The Psalmist adjures those who would be faithful to "Be still before the Lord, and wait patiently for him" (37:7 NRSV). Charles stresses the role of humble faith in patience in his response to John 1:12, "to all who received him, who believed in his name, he gave power to become children of God" (NRSV).

> Not differing from a servant now,
> I wait in *humble faith,* till thou
> Art in my heart revealed:
> Then shall I Abba Father cry,
> An heir of all in earth and sky,
> An heir of glory sealed.[11]

Humble faith enables patience to wait until God is revealed in the heart. How long must one wait? No one knows, but humble faith is not impatient. Does this upset the so-called chronology of belief and faith? After one affirms that God is revealed to one's heart, is it not then that one is a person of faith? There can be many occurrences of God's revelation to human hearts. Charles affirms that one can be a person of humble faith who awaits the revelation of God in one's heart. The cry, "Abba, Father," is the affirmation that one senses God's revelation in the heart.

Charles expresses this affirmation in a different way, but it is intimately related to *humble faith.* It is not by some theological premise that he finds God's protection, but rather through God's name. When by *humble faith* he trusts in God's name, opposing forces can be left behind. It is through *humble faith* that he finds "The Lord my righteousness." It is just as though he cries again, "Abba, Father."

10. M. Casey, *Living in the Truth,* 5.

11. *SH* 1762, 2:239; based on John 1:12, "As many as received him, to them gave he power to become the sons of God, even to them that believe on his name" (KJV).

> Holy and just, I fly to thee,
> Thy name shall my protection be,
>   When guilty terrors press;
> I leave th' avenger far behind,
> Soon as by *humble faith* I find
>   The Lord my righteousness![12]

Humble faith has a strong eschatological significance, for it is a force that accompanies the faithful on earth and guides them to "the perfect day of love."

> Light of my soul, I follow thee,
> In *humble faith* on earth to see
>   Thy perfect day of love,
> And then with all thy saints in light
> To gain the beatific sight
>   Which makes their heaven above.[13]

---

12. *SH* 1762, 1:123; based on Joshua 20:7, "They appointed Kedesh [i.e., holy] in Galilee in Mount Napthali" (KJV).

13. *SH* 1762, 2:238–39; based on John 1:9, "That was the true Light, which lighteth every man that cometh into the world" (KJV).

Chapter 5: **Diverse Dimensions of Humility**

GIVEN THE STRONG EMPHASIS of the early church fathers/mothers and Charles Wesley on becoming God's nature, love, and bearing God's nature in life, it is not surprising that Wesley wrestles with diverse aspects of how human beings personify God's humility. There are many aspects of human behavior that are in conflict with being humble. How can one's demeanor reflect humility? Charles pleads with himself—

> Humble, and teachable, and mild,
> O may I, as a little child,
>   My lowly Master's steps pursue:
> Be anger to my soul unknown,
> Hate, envy, jealously be gone!
>   In love create thou all things new.[1]

The opening word of the stanza, which is "humble," sets the tone for every aspect of his demeanor mentioned in these lines. It is as though the words "humble" and "love" serve as "bookends" of all dimensions of his behavior mentioned here. As someone who is humble, he is teachable and mild. He seeks to follow in the steps of the Master, and therefore he is to be devoid of hate, envy, and jealously, and in love all things are created new.

---

1. *HSP* 1740, 46.

Charles's lines remind one of St. John Climacus' comment: "As with the appearance of light, darkness retreats; so, at the fragrance of humility, all anger and bitterness vanish."[2]

The Problem of Pride

Just two years later, in 1742, after the appearance of the above lines by Charles, he published *Hymns on God's Everlasting Love,* in which he prayerfully pleads:

> O! Do not let me trust
> In any arm but thine,
> Humble, O humble to the dust
> This stubborn soul of mine:
> Cast all my reeds aside,
> Captivate every thought,
> And drain me of my strength and pride,
> And bring me down to nought.[3]

Charles pleads to be drained of pride, for he realizes that it is one of the main enemies of humility. Pride is opposed to humility. In a poem titled "A Prayer for Humility" pride pursues the very thing which is God's gift to all in Christ, namely, grace.

> As the substance by the shade,
> Grace I find by pride pursued;
> Grace is pride's occasion made,
> Evil ever cleaves to good.[4]

St. Diadochos of Photiki[5] (c. 400–before c. 486) writes of a man with a desire that God should be glorified in him, and in contrast he should see himself as nothing.

2. Climacus, *The Ladder of Divine Ascent.* Step 8: "On Freedom from Anger and On Meekness."

3. *HGEL* 1742, 37.

4. *HSP* 1742, 32.

5. St. Diadochos was bishop of Photiki and participated in the Council of Chalcedon (451). One of his best known works is "On the Contemplative Life." He is known to have greatly influenced Maximos the Confessor, John Climacus, and Symeon the New Theologian.

This man does not think of what he is, even when others praise him. In his great desire for humility he does not think of his priestly rank, but performs his ministry as the rules enjoin. In his extreme love for God, he strips himself of any thought of his own dignity; and with a spirit of humility he buries in the depths of divine love any pride to which his high position might give rise. Thus, out of desire to humble himself, he always sees himself in his own mind as a useless servant, extraneous to the rank he holds. We too should do the same, fleeing all honor and glory in the overflowing richness of our love for the Lord who loves us so greatly.[6]

There is a grave danger of one boasting of grace received, which results in poverty, forsakenness, and aloneness. Is it possible that one can be proud of one's own humility? Apparently this is something Wesley fears.

> When the boasted grace is gone,
>   Humbled in the dust I lie,
> Poor, forsaken, and alone,
>   From the deep on God I cry,
> Seeing there my loss of God,
>   Proud I am my loss to see,
> Proud to find that I am proud,
>   Proud of my humility.[7]

There is a "self-preferring love" that stands in the way of humility. Charles offers a prayer for its removal.

> Jesus, out of our hearts remove
> The bane of self-preferring love,
> Which odious in thy saints appear[s],
> Most odious in thy ministers:
> Let each confess with humble shame,
> I nothing have, I nothing am:
> The least of saints with pity see,
> The chief of sinners save in me.[8]

6. *Philokalia*, 1:256.

7. *HSP* 1742, 32.

8. *SH* 1762, 2:408; based on 3 John 9, "Diotrephes loveth to have the

In concert with a number of the early church fathers, Wesley sees pride as a demon that destroys human goodness.

> O the curse, the plague I feel
> By the demon pride pursued!
> Proud to see I merit hell,
> Proud I am that God is good.
>
> . . .
>
> O forbid it humble love!
> Hide me, O my Father, hide,
> Far away this snare remove,
> Save me from the demon pride.[9]

In volume 1 of the *Philokalia* one reads: "Nor will one escape pride, the first offspring of the devil, unless one has banished avarice, the root of all evil, since poverty makes a man humble, according to Solomon (cf. Prov. 10:4.). In short, no one can fall into the power of any demon, unless he has been wounded by those of the front line."[10] The passage goes on to say that this is why the devil tempted Jesus in the wilderness. One can drive the devil away only by rejection of the offered temptations (cf. Matthew 4:1–11).

Charles Wesley has an ongoing struggle with humility and pride. On Saturday, July 19, 1740, he wrote (note his shorthand comment within double brackets, which was his later addition):

> After the morning exposition [I] prayed with the poor returning prodigals, who will—all of them, I trust—once more escape out of the snare of the devil. From 9:00 to 12:00 employed in reading the letters. When I see what God has done by me, it even confounds me [but in the next moment I found I am proud of my humility[11]].

---

preeminence" (KJV).

9. *HSP* 1742, 149–50.

10. *Philokalia*, 1:38.

11. This shorthand comment was added by Charles Wesley between the lines of text.

Dined at Mr. [Thomas] Willis's[12] and read a sermon of Tobias Crisp's.[13] Whether he be an antinomian as supposed, I know not. But this I know, that he denies Christian holiness, as do all the Puritans (whom I have met with) to a man. This does not make me anything readier to swallow their blessed doctrine of predestination.[14]

In an answer to a letter from Wales on September 6, 1740, he wrote:

My lot has been to meet with treachery and ingratitude from almost every one I ever loved. I can *forgive* such, but not *trust* them. In returning them good for evil I find no difficulty. But to humble myself before them, to follow them up with kindness so as even to seem *afraid* of them, this does much violence to my pride. That I compel myself to submit to it, and take up the cross my nature soul most abhors, whom my nature would soonest tear to pieces, those I labour first to put first into my bosom.[15]

In a lesser known text published in 1749 Charles reflected on his own being "as full of wrath and pride," which is opposed to the humility of God.

Gentle thou, and meek in heart,
All humility thou art;
Full of wrath, and pride I am,
How unlike my lowly Lamb.[16]

---

12. Charles Wesley was a frequent guest of Thomas Willis during this time, who apparently owned a coal mine in Hanham, about four miles east of Bristol city center. See Charles Wesley, *MSJ* 1:278, Sept. 22, 1740.

13. Tobias Crisp (1600–1643) was a strong Calvinist member of the Church of England clergy; a collection of his sermons was published at his death under the title *Christ Alone Exalted*, 1643.

14. Baker, Heitzenrater, Maddox, *The Journal Letters . . . Charles Wesley*, 57.

15. Baker, Heitzenrater, Maddox, *The Journal Letters . . . Charles Wesley*, 140–41.

16. *HSP* 1749, 2:161; stanza 3 of an eight-stanza poem based on Matthew 11:28–30.

Experiencing God's Humility

It is not surprising that Charles Wesley emphasizes that we experience God's humility. In a text titled "The Inward Cross" he declares: "I come, thy humbled state *to feel*." How so?—"to bear, and bleed, and die with thee."

> O my dear Master, and my Lord,
>   Good is thine acceptable will,
> I yield obeisance to thy word,
>   *I come, thy humbled state to feel,*
> My calling here I plainly see,
> To bear, and bleed, and die with thee.[17]

The Elder Josef[18] (1897–1957) also says something helpful about *feeling humility* when he avers, "Inner and real humility is for one to feel, that whatever he has, life, health, wealth, wisdom all are foreign, are gifts of God."[19] Humility is not merely an intellectual assent; it is an inner experience, which itself is a gift of God.

In the succeeding five stanzas of the poem by Wesley just cited, he describes how it is that he vicariously suffers with Christ. One is a person of grief who drinks the bitter cup of pain and cries out "Why hast thou forsaken me?" One suffers with Christ on the cross and at death sinks into his grave, but yet rises again, "The resurrection's power to prove / And live the life of perfect love." Through Christ's suffering one experiences the gift of humility. Yet one does well to recall Amma Theodora's[20] words

---

17. *HSP* 1749, 2:18.

18. Elder Joseph, though a twentieth-century monk at Mount Athos, as a Hesychast, his comments on humility are in the spirit of many of the early church fathers/mothers. He was canonized a saint of the Eastern Orthodox Church in 2020.

19. "Elder Joseph the Hesychast" trans. from Greek by Elizabeth Theokrit-off, in *Mount Athos: The Great and Holy Monastery*, 195–98.

20. Not much is known about Amma Theodora except that she was part of a monastic community of women near Alexandria. It is reported that she advised Bishop Theophilus of Alexandria.

"that neither asceticism nor vigils nor any kind of suffering are able to save, only true humility can do that."[21]

The experience of humility for Wesley is not passive. He speaks of an active humility, or a humility that is not still.

> Then let us agree our Jesus to praise:
> Come, triumph with me, and tell of his grace;
> No fear you shall stumble by doing his will,
> Be thankful and humble, but never be still.[22]

The last line, "Be thankful and humble, but never be still," does not sound like a quotation from the desert fathers, who cherished the opportunity to be still in meditation, prayer, and reflection. Charles's view is unquestionably bound with the ongoing active social engagement of the Methodist movement in eighteenth-century England, exemplified especially by his brother John, whether in establishing a medical dispensary for the poor at Westminster in London, helping those suffering from the dreadful conditions in work houses, or assisting with establishing a credit union for poor hearth workers in the coal industry.

In fact, both John and Charles Wesley could hardly be spoken of as thankful and humble priests of the Church of England who preferred being *still*, if to be still means the absence of social engagement. Indeed they experienced still moments of reflection and prayer, but these were often followed by active engagement, such as early morning Bible studies and prayer followed by visits to an Oxford prison during their university years.

Hence it is not surprising to find a very interesting use of "humble" as an adjective when Charles speaks of "humble zeal." One would not necessarily think of zealousness as being first and foremost humble. But in a poem titled "The Way of Duty the Way of Safety" in volume 1 of *HSP* 1749, Charles reflects on a laborer's twelve-hour days, and the conflicts faced. He says that though "Ten thousand snares my path beset"—

---

21. Ward, *The Sayings of the Desert Fathers*, 84.

22. *HSP* 1749, 1:231.

> Still will I strive, and labor still,
> With *humble zeal* to do thy will,
>   And trust in thy defense;
> My soul into thy hands I give,
> And, if he can obtain thy leave,
>   Let Satan pluck me thence.[23]

Clearly Charles understood that one can energetically, yet humbly, do God's will in the course of daily labor.

There is a more questionable use of this term "humble zeal" by Wesley in the *Thanksgiving Hymns* he published in 1759, amid the Seven Years' War, when he was pleading for God to intervene on behalf of the British to hold off a French invasion, which in fact the British did. Under the command of Admiral Edward Hawke the Channel Fleet of twenty-three ships held back the attack of a French fleet of twenty-two vessels. For the day of public thanksgiving on November 29, 1759, Wesley prepared a group of hymns with the title *Hymns to Be Used on the Thanksgiving Day, Nov. 29, 1759, and After It.* Hymn 12 bears the title "The Song of Moses,[24] Sung by Great Britain and Ireland, for the Victory Given Them over the French Fleet, Nov. the 20th, 1759." Stanza 2 of Hymn 12 reads:

> To him we will our trophies raise,
>   And chant his matchless powers:
> Our fathers' God, exalt his praise,
>   Our fathers' God is ours!
> Prepare his place with *humble zeal,*
>   Who takes his people's part;
> The Lord eternally shall dwell
>   In every faithful heart.[25]

Here I think that Wesley's loyalty to the English crown and his Tory tendencies have overtaken his humble faithfulness to God. It seems hardly appropriate to tell the people to be humbly zealous in believing that God had helped the British defeat the French. Even Charles's theology can occasionally take a wrong turn.

23. *HSP* 1749, 1:213.

24. See Exodus 15:1–18. *Thanksgiving Hymns* 1759, 27–28.

25. *Thanksgiving Hymns* 1759, 27–28.

In a contrasting passage which turns to one's inner vision of patience and humility, Charles writes in his *SH 1762*:

> True goodness grows on a good tree,
>   Meekness which no affront can move,
> Patience, *concealed* humility,
>   And all the fruits of *silent* love.[26]

The followers of Christ in their patience should exemplify a "*concealed* humility." It need not be acknowledged, i.e., make itself known, for it bears "the fruits of *silent* love." There is a quiet confidence that expresses itself in silent love. Not a word must be spoken.

Humility and the Mind

Given the diverse emphases related to humility already addressed in this chapter, it is not surprising that Charles Wesley speaks of the impact humility has on the mind. His first emphasis, however, is not to his own mind but to the mind of Christ. He desires the humble mind of Christ to be planted in us.

> Let the fruits of grace abound,
> Let in us thy bowels sound;

---

26. *SH 1762*, 1:216. This is part of a poem based on Luke 6:44, "Every tree is known by its own fruit" (KJV). In John's own copy of *SH 1762*, which Charles did not allow his brother to edit, John underlined the words "concealed humility" and "silent love" with an exclamation mark in the margin near "concealed humility." Randy L. Maddox comments: "I am confident John Wesley underlined these [words] because he disagreed with Charles; Charles was suggesting those who believed they had experienced Christian perfection should NOT speak of it; John encouraged them to do so, and called it a false or 'voluntary humility' that might lead them to stay silent." (Email, June 5, 2024).

Charles is clear, however, in a number of his poems that address "humility" that it is not something of which to be overtly proud or to boast. For references to John's use of "voluntary humility" see his correspondence in *John Wesley, Letters IV 1766–1773*, Vol. 28: "To Elizabeth (Patten) Bennis," August 14, 1766 (35); "To Philothea Briggs," May 13, 1772 (485) and October 19, 1772 (521–22). *John Wesley, Letters V 1774–1781*: "To Elizabeth Ritchie," November 12, 1776 (299–300).

Faith, and love, and joy increase,
Temperance and gentleness:

Plant in us thy *humble mind;*
Patient, pitiful, and kind.
Meek and lowly let us be,
Full of goodness, full of thee.[27]

This is the humble mind Wesley seeks: the humble mind of Christ to be planted in him and others. What is the humble mind of Christ like?—it is patient, pitiful, kind, meek, lowly, full of goodness, and full of God.

Charles anticipates this gift to all hearts and minds. It is the gift of the divine self in the humble, patient mind.

We wait, 'till thou the gift impart,
    The unction from above:
Come quickly, Lord, in every heart
    Set up thy throne of love.

Or, (for it is not ours to know
    The times by God assigned)
Give us, 'till thou thyself bestow,
    An humble patient mind.[28]

It is through the Incarnation that we experience the advent of humility. This then is how we know the mind of God. This is eloquently expressed in a poem of Charles not published during his lifetime.

'Tis here thy *mind* I know,
    Thy hidden kingdom see;
Thou com'st from heaven to reign below
    By deep humility;
    The High and Lofty One
    Thou dost our meanness bear:
And *by humility alone*
    Thy royal state we share.[29]

27. *HSP* 1740, 183.

28. *HSP* 1749, 2:326. These are stanzas 4 and 5 of a hymn of eight stanzas titled "Hymns for Christian Friends".

29. *UP* 2:80.

The Incarnation of God's humility both has an impact on and flows from the mind. Therefore, Charles does not grasp how a humble mind and a conceited mind can coexist.

> For how can contraries be joined,
> An humble with an *haughty* mind,
> Or two so different in degree,
> Descend, arise, and meet in thee?[30]

Nikitas Stithatos writes of humble-mindedness, which also emphasizes the impact of humility on the mind.

> We know ourselves to be participants in the Holy Spirit when we offer to God fruits worthy of the Spirit: love for God with all our soul and genuine love for our fellow beings, joy of heart issuing from a clear conscience; peace of soul as a result of dispassion and humility; generosity in our thoughts, long-suffering in affliction and times of trial, kindness and restraint in our behavior, deep-rooted unwavering faith in God, gentleness springing from *humble-mindedness* and compunction, and complete control of our senses.[31]

St. Makarius of Egypt[32] (c. 295–392) also emphasized the importance of humble-mindedness in his homily on "The Freedom of the Intellect."

> The abode and resting-place of the Holy Spirit is humility, love, gentleness, and the other holy commandments of Christ. If, therefore, a person desires to grow and to attain perfection by acquiring all these virtues, he must initially force himself to acquire and must establish himself in the first, that is to say, in prayer-wrestling and striving with his heart to make it receptive and obedient

30. *HSP* 1749, 2:260; the last four lines of stanza 5 of an eleven-stanza poem.

31. *Philokalia*, 1:164.

32. St. Makarius is one of the most important of the desert fathers of Scetis and is known for his strong emphasis on deification and some fifty homilies and seven Ascetic Treatises. Some of his prayers survive in the church today. There remain open questions regarding the authorship of the homilies attributed to his name.

to God. If he first forces himself in this way, completely subduing the resistance of his soul, through good habit making it obedient to him so that it joins with him in his prayer and supplication, then the grace of prayer that he has been given by the Spirit grows and flourishes, reposing upon him together with humility, love and blessed gentleness which he has also sought to acquire. So, then, the Spirit grants him these virtues as well, teaching him the *true humility*, genuine love and gentleness that he has previously impelled himself to ask for. Thus he grows and is made perfect in the Lord, and is found worthy of the kingdom of heaven. For the humble man never falls: where, indeed, can he fall to if he regards himself as lower than all things? While lofty-mindedness leads to great humiliation, *humble-mindedness* on the contrary is a great and highly exalted glory.[33]

It is quite interesting to find Charles Wesley using some of the same language as Macarius, when he speaks of the importance of *true humility.* The opposite of true humility is, of course, false humility, which the early church fathers and mothers often address and of which Charles Wesley quite candidly speaks. He asks a most interesting question: how can one assume the lowest place when one "glories in the heights of grace"? Is one not to rejoice in the awareness of God's overwhelming act of grace in the Incarnation on behalf of all humankind? One must have an awareness of one's pride, if one is to experience *true humility.*

> How does he take the lowest place
> Who glories in the heights of grace,
> And free from self-mistrusting fear
> Assumes the perfect character?
> If void of *true humility,*
> No place among the saints hath he;
> And if his pride he will not feel,
> Shall have the lowest place—in hell.[34]

33. *Philokalia,* 3:346. "St Symeon Metaphrastis' Paraphrase of the Homilies of St Makarios of Egypt."

34. *SH* 1762, 2:225, based on Luke 14:10: "Sit down in the lowest room" (KJV).

Macarius avers, however, that "the humble man never falls. For whence should he fall, who is below all? Self-elevation is great abasement: but self-abasement is a great exaltation, and honor, and dignity."[35] He is convinced that humility "is the very sign of Christianity. . . . But if anyone say, I am satisfied, I am full, this is a deceiver and a liar."[36]

35. *Primitive Morality: Or, The Spiritual Homilies of St. Macarius the Egyptian.* London: W. Taylor, 1721, 290.

36. *Primitive Morality*, 240–41.

Chapter 6: Congruences in the Thoughts of Charles Wesley on Humility and Those of St. Basil the Great in His *Homily on Humility*

Thus far, many similarities of Charles Wesley's views on humility with those of the early church tradition have been observed. There is, however, a document of St. Basil the Great (330–379), bishop of Caesarea Mazaca in Cappadocia, Asia Minor, namely, his *Homily on Humility*, in which there is astonishing agreement on the subject of humility between these two important figures of Christian history, though they are centuries apart. While a specific date for Basil's homily has never been determined, Mark DelColgiano suggests that "it cannot be dated more precisely than to the entire span of Basil's ecclesiastical ministry, 362–378."[1]

Basil's homily has seven sections, and it is most interesting that what Basil has to say in each section resonates with Charles Wesley in diverse poetry and prose. While Wesley does not say precisely what is very important to Basil, namely, that humility saves humankind from the fall, the former affirms time and again that it is the humility of God born in the Incarnation that alone is the source of salvation.

---

1. DelColgiano, *St. Basil the Great*, 108. The quotations from St. Basil's *Homily on Humility* are taken from the translation that appears in DelCogliano's volume *St. Basil the Great On Christian Doctrine and Practice*, 2012.

> The Ancient of Days
> To redeem a lost race,
> From his glory comes down
> Self-humbled to carry us up to a crown.[2]

As Basil states: "And so, the great salvation for him [man, human being], both the remedy for his illness and the road back to his original estate, is humility, not imagining that the ornament of glory is attained through himself but seeking it instead from God."[3]

False Pride

In section 1 Basil affirms that the hope of false glory and haughtiness leads to vanity and pride. He mentions numerous things which lead to both: money, fancy food, ostentatious clothing, sumptuous feasts, beautiful objects, and privileged rank. Those who treasure these things "act as if they have transcended human nature."[4]

In the following poem Wesley covers a number of the subjects addressed by Basil, particularly pride, rank, wealth, honor, money, and power. These are some of the things with which those who are "self-exalting worms" seek "to magnify" themselves. Wesley prays that God will "stay the plague of pride."

> O Thou who dost the proud withstand,
> While those that stoop beneath thy hand,
>   Thy hand sets up on high,
> Behold the men whose load we bear
> Who, sprung out of the dunghill, dare
>   Themselves to magnify.
>
> The *self-exalting* worms abase,
> *Ambitious of the highest place,*

---

2. *HNL* 1745, 11, Hymn 8, stanza 4.

3. DelColgiano, *St. Basil the Great,* 108.

4. Ibid.

Into the lowest thrust,
Compelled to feel thine angry frown;
   Their Luciferian pride cast down
      And humble to the dust.

Down to the dust, but not to hell,
Abase the men who long have fell
   From their humility,
Who now at wealth and honor aim
Audacious for their own to claim
   The sheep redeemed by thee.

Wild havoc of the flock they make
For power and filthy lucre's sake
   And into parties rend,
Unless thy mercy interpose
And save thy people from their foes
   And save them to the end.

Our gracious and almighty Lord,
According to thy faithful word
   In which thy Church confide,
Stand thou before the poison spread
Betwixt the living and the dead
   And *stay the plague of pride.*

Now, now the dire contagion stop,
The source of bitter strife dry up,
   The stumbling block remove,
That all may think and speak the same
And breathe the Spirit of the Lamb
   In meek and lowly love.[5]

At the beginning of the second section of Basil's *Homily on Humility* he says, "Of all the goods possessed by human beings, the one which appears to be the greatest and most reliable is wisdom and prudence. Yet even this is liable to vain haughtiness and may not result in true exaltation. For these count for nothing

5. *UP* 3:77–78.

when the wisdom that comes from God is lacking." This theme is continued in section 3.

> No one who is prudent will have a high opinion of himself on account of either his own wisdom or the other things mentioned above. Instead, he will comply with the excellent advice offered by the blessed Anna and the prophet Jeremiah. "Let not the wise man boast in his wisdom, nor the powerful man boast in his power, nor the rich man in his riches" [Jer. 9:23]. But what is true boasting? And what makes a person truly great? He says: "Let him who boasts boast in this: that he understands and knows that I am the Lord" [Jer. 9:24].[6]

Charles Wesley's comments based on Jeremiah 9:23 in his lyrical commentary *SH 1762* resonate with those of Basil. Charles's first line is essentially a quotation from the Jeremiah verse.

> *Let not the wise his wisdom boast,*
>   The mighty glory in his might,
> The rich in flattering riches trust
>   Which take their everlasting flight;
> The rush of numerous years beats down
>   The most gigantic strength of man,
> And where is all his wisdom gone,
>   When dust, he turns to dust again![7]

Lines 5 through 8 of this stanza sound very much like Basil's own words: "Furthermore, a person can be cocky on account of the power of his hands and the swiftness of his feet and the elegance of his body—things which are ravaged by illness and plundered by time. Such a person does not realize that 'all flesh is grass, and all the glory of man is like the flower of grass; the grass has withered and the flower has fallen' [Isa. 40:6]."[8]

Wesley's poem continues:

6. DelColgiano, *St. Basil the Great*, 112.

7. *SH* 1762, 2:16; based on Jeremiah 9:23, "Let not the wise man glory in his wisdom," etc. (KJV).

8. DelColgiani, *St Basil the Great*, 110.

> One only gift can justify
>   The boasting soul that knows his God,
> When Jesus doth his blood apply,
>   I glory in his sprinkled blood,
> The Lord my righteousness I praise,
>   I triumph in the love divine,
> The wisdom, wealth, and strength of grace,
>   In Christ, through endless ages mine.

Basil emphasizes the perils of boasting and pride: "Paul boasts because he despises his own righteousness and seeks 'that which comes through Christ, the righteousness from God through faith, that he may know him and the power of his resurrection, and may share his sufferings by becoming like him in his death, if somehow he may attain the resurrection of the dead' [Phil. 3.9–11]. By this is every exaltation of pride laid low."[9]

Charles Wesley makes a strong statement on the theme of boasting and pride based on Philippians 3:12, "Not as though I . . . were already perfect," in which he writes some rather sarcastic lines that make fun of those who take pride in their conceit.

> "Then know thy place, (a novice cries,
> Whose fancy has attained the prize)
> "Stand by thyself, nor rank with me,
> "For I am holier than thee;
> "Beyond the chief apostle I!
> "And you, who dare my grace deny,
> "The proof of my perfection know,
> "It is—because I *think* it so!"[10]

What selfish pride!— do not "rank with me" . . . "I am holier" . . . I am "beyond the chief apostle." What is the proof of these things? "I *think* it so!"

Reflecting on Philippians 2:3, "In lowliness of mind let each esteem other better than themselves" (KJV), Charles writes:

9. DelColgiano, *St. Basil the Great,* 112. DelColgiani notes that Basil has slightly altered the verbs in the scriptural passage from first person to third person singular.

10. *SH* 1762, 2:316; based on Philippians 3:12, "Not as though I . . . were already perfect" (KJV).

> Proclaiming my own holiness,
>   Myself if perfect I esteem,
> And others far beneath in grace;
>   Myself I must prefer to them.[11]

Isidore of Pelusium[12] (d. c. 450) offers sound advice: "The heights of humility are great and so are the depths of boasting. I advise you to attend to the first and not to fall into the second."[13]

Wesley knows there is a different response for the faithful follower of Jesus. After reading Philippians 3:12, "I follow after, if that I may apprehend that for which also I am apprehended of Christ Jesus" (KJV), he wrote:

> Jesus, that perfect good unknown,
>   Restless, resigned, I wait to gain:
> But give me strength to follow on,
>   And strive, and labor, and sustain;
> Nor ever from thine own depart,
>   'Till thee I love with all my heart.[14]

Humility and Self-aggrandizement: The Publican and the Pharisee

Basil's homily turns next to 1 Corinthians 15:10, and he comments: "God grants efficacy to our toils; Paul says, 'I worked harder than all of them, yet not I but the grace of God with me."[15] Basil acknowledges that Paul takes no credit for his diligence and hard work, but rather he knows that all is by God's grace alone.

---

11. *SH* 1762, 2:316, based on Philippians 2:3, "In lowliness of mind let each esteem other better than themselves" (KJV).

12. Though born in Egypt to a prominent Alexandrian family, Isidore of Pelusium became known as an ascetic and moved to a mountain near the city of Pelusium. He is known particularly for his letters to Cyril of Alexandria.

13. Ward, *The Sayings of the Desert Fathers*, 98.

14. *SH* 1762, 2:317, based on Philippians 3:12, "I follow after, if that I may apprehend that for which also I am apprehended of Christ Jesus" (KJV).

15. DelCogliano, *St. Basil the Great*, 112.

Similarly, Charles Wesley responds to the same 1 Corinthians passage in this way:

> O for that *just* humility
> Which gives whate'er is good to thee,
> Teaches thine instrument to cry
> The Lord he doth the work, not I!
> Take all the glory of thy grace,
> Take all the everlasting praise![16]

Charles maintains: it is "*just* humility" that teaches us to affirm: "The Lord he doth the work, not I!" It is to God that glory and everlasting praise are due.

In the fourth section of Basil's homily he asks: "Why are you haughty as if what you have comes from yourself? . . . You have not come to know God through your righteousness, but God has come to know you through kindness. He says: 'You have come to know God, or rather to be known by God' [Galatians 4:9]. You have not embraced Christ through your virtue, but Christ has embraced you through his advent."[17] A related passage to which Basil and Charles Wesley both refer is John 15:16, "You did not choose me," says the Lord, "but I chose you" (NRSV). Here is Wesley's response to the text, which is quite similar to Basil's interpretation.

> Thee we never could have chose,
>   Dead in sins and trespasses:
> But thou hast redeemed thy foes,
>   Bought the universal peace,
> That all our ransomed race might prove
> The sweetness of electing love.[18]

Basil is deeply concerned with self-aggrandizement and turns to Paul's letter to the Romans for illumination. "Is it because you have been honored that you think highly of yourself and take

16. *SH* 1762, 2:295; based on 1 Corinthians 15:10, "Yet not I, but the grace of God which was with me" (KJV).

17. DelCogliano, *St. Basil the Great*, 113.

18. *SH* 1762, 2:261; based on John 15:16, "Ye have not chosen me, but I have chosen you" (KJV).

these acts of mercy as occasions of pride? In that case, know yourself, recognize who you are: Adam banished from paradise, Saul abandoned by the Spirit of God, Israel severed from the holy root. He says: 'By faith you have stood firm, do not be proud but fear' [Romans 11.20]."

The English text Charles Wesley used for Romans 11:20 reads "Be not high-minded, but fear" (KJV). Therefore he begins with the idea of high-mindedness.

> Nature's high-mindedness
> How shall I lay aside?
> I cannot, Lord, myself abase,
> Myself divest of pride:
> But if thou speak the word,
> The word imparts the fear,
> And poor, and vile, and self-abhorred
> I at thy feet appear.

Wesley continues:

> Here let me ever lie
> And tremble at thy grace,
> Afraid to meet thy pitying eye,
> To see thy smiling face:
> Thus only may I prove
> My growth in grace sincere,
> And calmly wait, till perfect love
> Complete my humble fear.[19]

Basil turns to the story of the Pharisee and the tax-collector in Luke 18:11–14. "Furthermore, that Pharisee, who was overbearing and excessively proud, who not only was cocky on account of his righteousness but also disparaged the tax-collector who was standing before God, lost the righteousness in which he could boast because of his sin of pride."[20]

Charles Wesley also responds to this story with a stinging indictment of the Pharisee.

---

19. *SH* 1762, 2:284; based on Romans 11:20, "Be not high-minded, but fear" (KJV).

20. DelCogliano, *St. Basil the Great*, 114.

The modern Pharisee is bold
In boasting to surpass the old:
Triumphant in himself, he stands
Conspicuous with extended hands,
With hideous screams and outcries loud
Proclaims his goodness to the crowd,
Glories in his own perfect grace,
And blasphemies presents for praise!
"Again I thank thee, and again,
"That I am not as other men,
"But holy as thyself, and pure
"And must, O God, like thee endure:
"Thyself I now to witness call,
"That I am good, and cannot fall,
"Thee to exalt, repeat the word,
"And thus I glory—in the Lord!"[21]

John Chrysostom is of like mind in his interpretation of the story.

> Though fasting, prayer, almsgiving, temperance, any
> other good things whatever, be gathered together in you;
> without humility all fall away and perish. It was this very
> thing that took place in the instance of the Pharisee. For
> even after he had arrived at the very summit, he went
> down [Luke 18:14] with the loss of all, because he had
> not the mother of virtues: for as pride is the fountain of
> wickedness, so is humility the principle of self-command.
> Wherefore also he [Christ] begins with this, pulling up
> boasting by the very root out of the soul of his hearers.[22]

Basil picks up the story: "For the tax-collector glorified the
holy God and did not even dare to lift up his eyes, but sought only
mercy, accusing himself by his posture, by beating his breast, and
by seeking nothing other than mercy."[23]

21. *UP* 2:169; based on Luke 18:11, "God, I thank thee that I am not as
other men are," etc. (KJV).

22. *Homily 15 on Matthew*. Advent: https://www.newadvent.org/fathers/
200115.htm; accessed February 11, 2024.

23. DelCogliano, *St. Basil the Great*, 114.

Wesley also pays due homage to the tax-collector in his response to Luke 18:13. "And the publican, standing afar off, would not lift up so much as his eyes unto heaven" (KJV).

> A penitent indeed
> Has nothing good to plead,
> Guilt confesses with his eyes,
> Dares not lift them up to heaven,
> Not so much in words, as sighs
> Prays, and begs to be forgiven.
>
> O'erwhelmed with conscious fear
> He trembles to draw near;
> Far from the most holy place,
> Far from God his distance keeps,
> Feels his whole unworthiness,
> Feels—but shame has sealed his lips.
>
> Labors his struggling soul
> With indignation full;
> With unuttered grief oppresed,
> Grief too big for life to bear,
> Self-condemned he smites his breast,
> Smites his breast—and God is there!
>
> Loosed by the power of grace,
> Behold, at last he prays!
> Pleads th'atoning sacrifice
> For mere sin and misery,
> Humbly in the Spirit cries,
> "God be merciful to me!"[24]

Basil continues with the story: it was "the tax-collector rather than the Pharisee who went down [to his house] made righteous." Luke 18:14, "I tell you, this man went down to his house justified rather than the other" (KJV). Of the tax-collector

---

24. UP 2:169–70; based on Luke 18:13, "The publican, standing afar off, would not lift up so much as his eyes unto heaven" (KJV).

he says, "It is often the case that humility saves a person who has committed many serious sins."[25]

> Jesus doth the truth declare;
> The boaster bears his load,
> Hastning from the house of prayer
> Beneath the curse of God:
> God the publican receives;
> And conscious of the blood applied,
> He with joy the temple leaves,
> A sinner justified.

> God resists the proud and vain
> Of their own righteousness,
> Every self-exalting man
> Almighty to abase:
> All themselves who justify
> He dooms his endless wrath to feel,
> Bold invaders of the sky
> He *brings* them down to hell.

> Sinners self-condemned he cheers
> With blessings from above,
> Grace, abundant grace confers,
> And sweet forgiving love;
> Strangely condescends to stoop,
> And dwell with every contrite one,
> Lifts the humbled mourner up,
> And seats him on his throne.[26]

Self-confidence: Peter's Case

Basil also addresses a very difficult issue by commenting on Peter's claim to Jesus that he will never deny him. "I myself nonetheless will never fall away [Matthew 26:33]." Basil comments further: "Because of this he [Peter] was delivered over to human cowardice

25. DelCogliano, *St. Basil the Great*, 115.

26. *UP* 2, 170–71; based on Luke 18:14, "I tell you, this man went down to his house justified, rather than the other" (KJV).

and fell into denying the Lord."[27] Was Peter's claim one of which he was to boast? Was it something of which to be proud?

Charles Wesley is also concerned with the peril of a self-righteous claim in reference to Peter. After reading the text: "Though all men shall be offended because of thee, yet will I never be offended" (Matthew 26:33 KJV), he wrote:

> One moment, Lord, if thou depart,
>   With like presumption I
> Shall trust my own deceitful heart,
>   And give my God the lie:
> Though all prove faithful to thy cause,
>   Without thy constant power,
> I only stumbling at thy cross
>   Shall fall, and rise no more.[28]

Charles then continues responding specifically to the passage cited by Basil, "Though I should die with thee, yet will I not deny thee" (Matthew 26:35 KJV).

> Who trust in a supposed decree,
> Or your own perfect purity,
>   And cannot fall from grace,
> Before your Master you deny,
> Before you curse your God and die,
>   Remember Peter's case![29]

Both Basil and Wesley are asking us to "Remember Peter's case!"

We come next to the fifth section of Basil's *Homily on Humility*. It continues a discussion of how we view ourselves. He begins by saying:

> Do you think you have accomplished something good? Give thanks to God lest you exalt yourself above your neighbor. He says: "Let each one test his own work, and then his reason to boast will be in himself alone and not

27. DelCogliano, *St. Basil the Great*, 114.

28. *SH* 1762, 2:191; based on Matthew 26:33, "Though all men shall be offended because of thee, yet will I never be offended" (KJV).

29. *SH* 1762, 2:191; based on Matthew 26:35, "Thou I should die with thee, yet will I not deny thee" (KJV).

in another" [Gal 6.4]. . . . In general, remember that true proverb: "God resists the proud but he gives grace to the humble" [Prov 3.34]. Keep this word of the Lord near: "Everyone who humbles himself will be exalted and everyone who exalts himself will be humbled" [Luke 14.11].[30]

Wesley's response to Luke 14:11 is in two parts. (1) "Whosoever exalteth himself shall be abased" (KJV). Here he personalizes the text by writing in the first person.

Why have I, Lord, so often been
Baffled, debased by every sin?
  With humble shame and grief
One sin I own the cause of all,
Pride always went before my fall,
  The pride of unbelief.[31]

(2) "He that humbleth himself shall be exalted."

Give me, O Lord, my soul t' abase,
To sink o'erwhelmed with pardning grace
  Lower and lower yet;
But till I mount above the skies,
O may I never, never rise
  From weeping at thy feet![32]

"Sink Me to Perfection's Height"

Basil begins the sixth section of his homily by admonishing us to "combat our pride." "Let us lower ourselves to exalt ourselves, imitating the Lord who descended from heaven into extreme humility and in turn was raised up from humility to an appropriate exaltation. Indeed, we find that everything the Lord did is a lesson in humility."[33] Basil then reiterates a litany of Christ's practice

30. DelCogliano, *St. Basil the Great*, 115.

31. *SH* 1762, 2:225; based on Luke 14:11, "Whosoever exalteth himself shall be abased" (KJV).

32. *SH* 1762, 2:225; based on Luke 14:11, "He that humbleth himself shall be exalted" (KJV).

33. DelCogliano, *St. Basil the Great*, 116.

of humility throughout his life from his infancy to his shameful death on a cross.

Resonating with Basil's comment "Let us lower ourselves to exalt ourselves," consider some words of Charles Wesley cited earlier in this study.

> Assert thy claim, receive thy right,
>   Come quickly from above,
> And *sink* me to perfection's height,
>   The *depth of humble love*.[34]

Though one may think of progressing toward and rising to "perfection's height," Wesley says precisely the opposite: "And *sink* me to perfection's height, / The *depth of humble love*."

If with Basil we remember that "everything the Lord did is a lesson in humility," the celebration of his life in and through the Christian year and the celebration of the sacraments which in themselves are a journey through everything he did, we are celebrating, participating in, and practicing Christ's lessons in humility. Christ's lessons in humility "are for us divine lessons passed down by our fathers [/mothers]. Come, let us imitate them, so that out of our humility there may arise for us everlasting glory, the perfect and true gift of Christ."[35]

In section 7 Basil returns to the subject of pride, which is also found in section 1. He asks:

> So then, how shall we descend to saving humility and be rid of the malignant tumor of pride? If we practice humility in everything and do not neglect anything as if no harm could come to us from it. For the soul grows like what it pursues, and is molded and shaped according to what it does. Your appearance, and your garments, and your transportation, and your table, and your chairs, and the style of your meals, and your bed and bedding, and your house, and the furnishings in your house: all of these should reflect thrift. And your speaking, and your singing, and your conversations

34. *HSP* 1749, 1:164.
35. DelCogliano, *St. Basil the Great*, 117.

with your neighbor: these too should look to modesty rather than to pretentiousness.[36]

Basil maintains that these things should reflect thrift, and one should prefer modesty over pretentiousness. He uses a series of scripture passages[37] to illustrate the biblical support of his position.

In his response to 1 Peter 5:5, "God resisteth the proud, and giveth grace to the humble" (KJV), Charles Wesley also takes a strong position against pride, with which this author believes is compatible with Basil's views:

> Vain of your gifts and boasted grace,
>   Great things who of yourselves declare,
> From you the Lord shall hide his face,
>   And leave you in the fowler's snare
> A wretched, self-deceiving crowd,
> False saints, false-witnesses, for God.

> Against your Luciferian pride
>   His furious jealously shall burn,
> And while you in the flesh confide,
>   Your towering confidence o'erturn,
> Into the flaming dungeon cast,
> Or save you as by fire at last.

> But you that tremble at his frown,
>   And scarcely dare for mercy hope,
> Your God in justice casts you down,
>   Your God in love shall lift you up,
> And bless and gospelize the poor
> With pardon and salvation sure.

---

36. DelCogliano, *St. Basil the Great*, 117.

37. Proverbs 18:17, Job 31:34, Matthew 6:2 and 11:29, Galatians 6:1, and 1 Peter 4:11.

Pardoned, if you the grace retain,
    And deeper groan your wants increased;
The Lord shall visit you again,
    And ent'ring into perfect rest,
You live, when pride and self's destroyed,
Forever full, forever void.[38]

Those who boast of grace and declare great things of themselves shall find that God hides from them, and they become false saints, false witnesses. Such behavior is the sure path to destruction, however, though "God in justice casts you down, . . . God in love shall lift you up."[39] It is the visitation of God that destroys pride and egotism.

38. *SH* 1762, 2:395–96, based on 1 Peter 5:5, "God resisteth the proud, and giveth grace to the humble" (KJV).

39. Charles Wesley's mention of the poor as recipients of the gospel is an ongoing theme in his works. "And bless and gospelize the poor / With pardon and salvation sure."

Chapter 7: **Emulating Humility**

HOW DOES ONE EMULATE humility? Is humility something we can learn how to practice? Is saying "practice humility" self-contradictory? If one is consciously trying to practice humility, is that self-defeating? John Chrysostom stated quite plainly: "Though fasting, prayer, almsgiving, temperance, any other good thing whatever, be gathered in you; without humility all fall away and perish." Furthermore, he says, "Neither wealth, nor power, nor royalty itself, has so much power to exalt men, as the things which they possessed in all fullness." And "though you be a slave, a beggar, in poverty, a stranger, unlearned, there is nothing to hinder you from being blessed, if you emulate this virtue [humility]."[1]

What then is one to do? Is there no conscious way to practice humility? Must not one's cognitive skills be involved? At the same time, the emulation of humility is not merely a reflective exercise, though that may seem to be sufficient for some. Should not a holistic approach to humility be both passive and active, and involve the engagement of the mind and body? The difficulty is how to distinguish between self-betterment and self-enlightenment in this regard. Chrysostom, Basil, and Wesley give us lists of self-engagement which may be practiced with or without humility.

How do we learn to discern between self-serving humility, if it is even possible to say something so contradictory, and humility which issues from the desire to serve and sacrifice at all

1. *Homily 15 on Matthew.* Advent: https://www.newadvent.org/fathers/200115.htm; accessed February 11, 2024.

costs without acknowledgment or reward? Are there not humble gestures such as: the wealthy giving to the poor, food given to the hungry, clothing provided for the naked? What if even the free give freedom to the enslaved?

The problem is that the moment one feels the necessity to label one's own act or acts as humble, humility is completely lost. The emulation of humility leaves no room for self-praise or self-aggrandizement. Even a moment of self-evaluation can be deceptive. Was I humble or was I not? One should desire to be so filled with Christ's spirit of love, God's nature, which is love, that the question need not be asked. We give because Christ gave, and we love because Christ loved.

Even so, is there nothing that one can do to grow in the humility of Christ? How do we practice humility? We have learned from many early fathers/mothers of the church and Charles Wesley that we should avoid pride, do deeds of humble service, and speak avoiding sharp, castigating language. St. John Chrysostom cautions: "Though fasting, prayer, almsgiving, temperance, any other good thing whatever, be gathered together in you; without humility all fall away and perish."[2] Perhaps St. Basil provides a clue. As previously noted, he said that "everything that Christ did was a lesson in humility." Would a simplistic approach then be to do the things that Christ did so that one will be or can be humble? If one simply creates a list of repeatable humble acts, the goal of humility—to become God's nature, which is love, in thought, word, and deed—can be missed. Humility does not consist in the fulfillment of a list of humble acts.

What if practicing humility involved learning from Christ's lessons in humility? Again Basil said that "everything Christ did was a lesson in humility." Could it be that the liturgy of the church is a means of practicing humility? The cycle of the Christian year celebrates the lessons in humility of Christ's life. Beginning with Advent and Christmas, the Incarnation opens the vision to the self-humbling of God in the birth of Jesus. The church's liturgy invites the faithful to become recipients and stewards of God's

2. Chrysostom, *Homily 15 on Matthew*, 3.

self-humbling spirit. In addition, one encounters humble shepherds and eastern wise men, whose quest for a grasp of the humblest moment of divine intervention is celebrated time after time and into the season of Epiphany.

What is the season of Lent in preparation for Easter, but a lesson of lessons in humility, as the cross becomes the ultimate symbol of humility. Is one not practicing humility in observance of this? Is this yet another humility lesson of Christ? Could the stations of the cross during Lent be lessons in humility? There are many feast days celebrated by the church in which it re-enacts events and aspects of the life of Christ through Scripture, prayer, singing, and diverse observance, which can contribute to an authentic practice of humility. To these may be added certain saints days as well.

It is the liturgical practice of the lessons of humility in the life of Christ that can precipitate the overt life of humility's practice, which takes place without conscious awareness of performance.

The practice of Christ's lessons of humility through the liturgy of the church becomes the source of an individual's embodiment of humility. One does not need to be a follower of Christ to be a humble person or to perform acts of humility. However, it is precisely because everything Christ did was a lesson in humility that those who follow him and are consistent in their "reenactment" of what he did in his life, have the opportunity to learn afresh what humility means in his life and theirs. The idea of "re-enactment" is not to suggest becoming mini-Christs, doing everything he did. It means that by the constant remembrance and rehearsals of his lessons in humility there opens an option to personify and realize a humble life in life beyond the liturgy.

What do the liturgies of the church invite us to do?—to recall and enact: to preach good news to the poor, to proclaim release to the captives and recovering of sight to the blind, to set at liberty the oppressed, to heal the sick, to feed the hungry, and to eat with sinners. We do this in prayer, song, meditation, receiving bread and wine (the body and blood of Christ), knowing his life and action continue to serve as lessons of humility.

Of particular importance is the celebration of the Eucharist/ Holy Communion which incorporates all of the above. It is the ultimate reenactment of Christ's lessons in humility. It is not a liturgy of burial, but rather a liturgy of resurrection that summons all to a life of sacrificial humility. One departs the Eucharist in the awareness that Christ's life and sacrifice send all communicants forth to discover and enact a life of humility.

In chapter 1 of this study the first four lines of Charles Wesley's paraphrase of Psalm 131 were included. However, his complete paraphrase of the psalm is now included for the vision of a life posture of humility.

> Lord, if thou the grace impart,
> Poor in spirit, meek in heart,
> I shall as my Master be
> Rooted in humility.
>
> From the time that thee I know,
> Nothing shall I seek below,
> Aim at nothing great or high,
> Lowly both my heart and eye.
>
> Simple, teachable, and mild,
> Awed into a little child,
> Quiet now without my food,
> Weaned from ev'ry creature-good.
>
> Hangs my new-born soul on thee,
> Kept from all idolatry,
> Nothing wants beneath, above,
> Happy, happy in thy love.
>
> O that all might seek and find
> Every good in Jesus joined,
> Him let Israel still adore,
> Trust him, praise him evermore![3]

3. *CPH* 1743, 95.

Selected Bibliography

Alfeyev, Hilarion. *The Spiritual World of Isaac the Syrian.* Vol. 175. (Cistercian Studies Series) Trappist, KY, 2000.

Allchin, A. M. *Participation in God: A Forgotten Strand in Anglican Tradition.* Wilton, CT: Morehouse-Barlow, 1988. Also, "The Trinity in the Teaching of Charles Wesley: A Study in Eighteenth-Century Orthodoxy?" *Proceedings of The Charles Wesley Society.* 4:1997, 69–84.

Baker, Frank, Richard P. Heitzenrater, and Randy L. Maddox. *The Journal Letters and Related Biographical Items of The Rev. Charles Wesley, M.A.* Nashville: Kingswood/The Charles Wesley Society, 2018.

Bouteneff, Peter C. "All Creation in United Thanksgiving: Gregory of Nyssa and the Wesleys on Salvation," in *Orthodox and Wesleyan Spirituality,* 189–201.

Campbell, Ted A. *John Wesley and Christian Antiquity: Religious Vision and Cultural Change.* Nashville: Kingswood, 1999.

Carveley, Kenneth. "From Glory to Glory: The Renewal of All Things in Christ: Maximus the Confessor and John Wesley," in *Orthodox and Wesleyan Spirituality,* 173–88.

Casey, Michael. *Living the Truth: Saint Benedict's Teaching on Humility.* Liguori, MO: Liguori Publications, 1999.

Charlesworth, James H. "Two Similar Paths: Methodism and Greek Orthodoxy," in *Orthodox and Wesleyan Scriptural Understanding and Practice,* 107–29.

Christensen, Michael J., and Jeffrey Wittung, eds. *Partakers of the Life Divine.* Madison/Teaneck: Fairleigh Dickinson, 2007.

Chrysostom, John. *Homily 15 on Matthew.* Advent: https://www.newadvent.org/fathers/200115.htm.

Chryssavgis, John. "The Practical Way of Holiness: Isaiah of Scetis and John Wesley," in *Orthodox and Wesleyan Spirituality,* 81–99.

Climacus, John. *The Ladder of Divine Ascent.* Boston: Holy Transfiguration Monastery, 1978.

DelCogliano, Mark. *St. Basil the Great on Christian Doctrine and Practice.* Yonkers, NY: St. Vladimir's Seminary, 2012.

Delio, Ilia. *The Humility of God: A Franciscan Perspective*. Cincinnati, OH: Anthony Messenger, 2005.

Edmonson, Robert J., and Hal M. Helms, trans. and eds. *The Complete Fénélon*. Brewster, MA: Paraclete, 2008.

Ekonomtsev, Ioann. "Charles Wesley and the Hesychast Tradition," in *Orthodox and Wesleyan Spirituality*, 240.

Francis of Assisi. "A Letter to the Entire Order," in Delio, *The Humility of God*, 27–29.

Gill, John, ed. *Christ Alone Exalted* [52 Sermons of Tobias Crisp 1643]. *Complete and Unabridged*. Supralapsarian, 2014.

Golitzin, Alexander. *St Symeon the New Theologian On the Mystical Life: The Ethical Discourses*. Vol. 3. Crestwood, NY: Saint Vladimir's Seminary, 1997.

Grdzelidze, Tamara. "The Authority of Scriptural Interpretation: An Orthodox Perspective on the Positions of John Wesley and Modern Methodism," in *Orthodox and Wesleyan Scriptural Understanding and Practice*, 131–36.

Jillions, John A. "An Orthodox Reading of 1 Cor. 1:10–30: Any Room for Methodists?" In *Orthodox and Wesleyan Scriptural Understanding and Practice*, 43–63.

Kempis, Thomas à. *Humility and the Elevation of the Mind to God*. Trans. by Fr. Robert Nixon, OSB. Gastonia, NC: TAN, 2021.

Kimbrough, S T, Jr. *May She Have a Word With You?* Eugene, OR: Wipf and Stock, 2019.

———. Ed. *Orthodox and Wesleyan Spirituality*. Crestwood, NY: St. Vladimir's Seminary, 2000.

———. Ed. *Orthodox and Wesleyan Scriptural Understanding and Practice*. Crestwood, NY: St. Vladimir's Seminary, 2005.

———. Ed. *Orthodox and Wesleyan Ecclesiology*. Crestwood, NY: St. Vladimir's Seminary, 2007.

———. *Participation in the Life Divine*. Eugene, OR: Wipf and Stock, 2016.

———. Eds. S T Kimbrough, Jr., and Oliver A. Beckerlegge. *The Unpublished Poetry of Charles Wesley*. Vols. 2 and 3. Nashville: Kingswood, 1990, 1992.

Kishkovsky, Leonid. "The Wesleys' *Hymns on the Lord's Supper* and Orthodoxy." *Proceedings of The Charles Wesley Society*. 2:1995, 75–86.

Lossky, Nicholas. "Lancelot Andrewes: A Bridge Between Orthodoxy and the Wesley Brothers in the Realm of Prayer," in *Orthodox and Wesleyan Scriptural Understanding and Practice*, 149–56.

Louth, Andrew. *Introducing Eastern Orthodox Theology*. Downers Grove, IL: InterVarsity, 2013.

Maddox, Randy L. *Responsible Grace*. Nashville: Kingswood Books, 1994.

———. *Bicentennial Works of John Wesley, Letters IV 1766-1773*, Vol. 28. Ed. Randy L. Maddox, Nashville: Abingdon, 2023.

———. *Bicentennial Works of John Wesley, Letters IV 1774-1781*, Vol. 29. Ed. Randy L. Maddox, Nashville: Abingdon, 2023.

McVey, Kathleen, trans. *Ephrem the Syrian*. New York: Paulist, 1989.

Newport, Kenneth G. C. *The Sermons of Charles Wesley: A Critical Edition with Introduction and Notes*. Oxford: Oxford University, 2001.

———. *Charles Wesley: Life, Literature & Legacy*. Eds. Kenneth G. C. Newport and Ted A. Campbell. Peterborough, UK: Epworth, 2008.

Outler, Albert. *The "Platonism" of Clement of Alexandria*. Chicago: n.p., 1940.

———. *Augustine: Confessions and Enchiridion*. Philadelphia: Westminster, 1955.

———. *The Christian Tradition and the Unity We Seek*. New York: Oxford University, 1957.

———. *Historian and Interpreter of Christian Tradition*. Ed. Bob W. Parrott. The Albert Outler Library. Vol. 9. Anderson, IN: Bristol House, 1995.

Palmer, G. F. H.; Philip Sherrad; Kallistos Ware. *The Philokalia: The Complete Text Compiled by St Nikodimos of the Holy Mountain and St Makarios of Corinth*. Vols. 1–4. London/Boston: Faber and Faber, 1979, 1982, 1986, 1999.

Skoubourdis, Anna. *The Philokalia of the Holy Neptic Fathers*. Volume 5: compiled by St. Nikodemos of the Holy Mountain and St. Makarios of Corinth. Virgin Mary of Australia and Oceania, 2020.

Service Books of The Orthodox Church. Vol. 1. *The Divine Liturgy of St. John Chrysostom*. South Canaan, PA: St. Tikhon's Seminary, 1984

Theokritoff, Elizabeth. Trans. from Greek, "Elder Joseph the Hesychast" in *Mount Athos: The Great and Holy Monastery of Vatopaidi*, 1999, 195–98.

von Hildebrand, Dietrich. *Humility: Wellspring of Virtue*. Manchester, NH: Sophia Institute, 1976.

Wainwright, Geoffrey. "Trinitarian Theology and Wesleyan Holiness" in *Orthodox and Wesleyan Spirituality*, 59–80.

Wakefield, Gordon S. "John Wesley and Ephraem Syrus." *Hygoye: Journal of Syriac Studies*. 1:2, pp. 8, 12, 1998.

———. "Littérature du desert chez John Wesley." Irénikon 51:155–70, 1978.

Ward, Benedicta. *The Sayings of the Desert Fathers: The Alphabetical Collection*. Trappist, KY: Cistercian Publications, 1975,

Ware, Kallistos. *The Orthodox Way*. Crestwood, NY: St. Vladimir's Seminary Press, 1978.

Young, Frances. "Inner Struggle: Some Parallels Between the Spirituality of John Wesley and the Greek Fathers" in *Orthodox and Wesleyan Spirituality*, 157–72.

———. "God's Word Proclaimed: The Homiletics of Grace and Demand in John Chrysostom and John Wesley," in *Orthodox and Wesleyan Scriptural Understanding and Practice*, 137–48.

Selected Bibliography of Charles and John Wesley

Wesley, Charles

Funeral Hymns. London: [Strahan,] 1759.
Hymns and Sacred Poems. 2 Vols. Bristol: Farley, 1749.
Hymns for Children. Bristol: Farley, 1763.
Hymns for the Nativity of Our Lord. London: [Strahan], 1745.
Hymns for Those That Seek and Those That Have Redemption in the Blood of Christ. London: Strahan, 1747.
Hymns on God's Everlasting Love. London: Strahan, 1742.
Hymns to be Used on the Thanksgiving Day, Nov. 29, 1759, and After it. [London: Strahan, 1759].
Short Hymns on Select Passages of the Holy Scriptures. 2 Vols. Bristol: Farley, 1762.
The Unpublished Poetry of Charles Wesley. 3 Vols., edited by S T Kimbrough, Jr., and Oliver A. Beckerlegge. Nashville: Abingdon/Kingswood, 1988, 1990, 1992.

Wesley, John and Charles Wesley

Hymns and Sacred Poems. London: Strahan, 1739.
Hymns and Sacred Poems. London: Strahan, 1740.
Hymns and Sacred Poems. Bristol: Farley, 1742.
Hymns on the Lord's Supper. Bristol: Farley, 1745.

Wesley, John

A Collection of Psalms and Hymns, 2nd ed. London: Strahan, 1743.
A Collection of Hymns for the Use of the People Called Methodists. Eds. Franz Hildebrandt and Oliver A. Beckerlegge. *Works of John Wesley*, Vol. 7. Oxford: Oxford University, 1983.

87

Index of Personal Names

Index of Scripture Passages

www.ingramcontent.com/pod-product-compliance
Lightning Source LLC
Chambersburg PA
CBHW060417090426
42734CB00011B/2346